The Impossible Team

The Worst to First
Patriots' Super Bowl Season

Nick Cafardo

TRIUMPH
B O O K S
CHICAGO

Library of Congress Cataloging-in-Publication Data

Cafardo, Nick.
    The impossible team : the worst to first Patriots' Super Bowl season
    / Nick Cafardo.
      p. cm.
    Includes index.
    ISBN 1-57243-494-5 (hc.)
    1. New England Patriots (Football team)—History. I. Title.

GV956.N36 C34 2002
796.332'64'0974461—dc21

                                  2002069553

This book is available in quantity at special discounts for your group or organization. For further information, contact:

Triumph Books
601 South LaSalle Street
Suite 500
Chicago, Illinois, 60605
(312) 939-3330
Fax (312) 663-3557

Printed in the United States of America
ISBN 1-57243-494-5
Interior design by Patricia Frey
All photos courtesy of AP/Wide World Photos

Dedicated to the memory of
George Martin Wood

Contents

Foreword

I've been with the Patriots through thick and thin for nine years. I always had a sense of when I was going to be a part of a good team, and I believed it from the start with the 2001 Patriots.

While nobody thought we were that good when we arrived at training camp in Smithfield, Rhode Island, in late July 2001, we all had a feeling there was a good group of people working hard toward a common goal. I could sense we were going to be a good team.

We had veteran players who had been through the NFL wars either here in New England or with other teams. They were players I had played against and respected. Most of them had played for Bill Belichick in New York, so they understood immediately what was expected of them, and they taught the guys who didn't know Bill all about the system he had in place.

We needed depth, and we got it. The front office did a great job filling all of the needs we had after 2000. We drafted some good players in Richard Seymour and Matt Light, and we added good, hardworking people who were dedicated to winning.

I knew what my responsibility was. I needed to make plays both as a receiver and a punt returner. That's what I get paid to do. That's my role. I also wanted to win more than anyone. I didn't get to play in the Super Bowl in 1997 because of an injury, which was tremendously disappointing to me. And then we lost the game and that was even more disappointing.

I wanted to get back.

We had some down years and it was hard for a lot of people to imagine we'd ever get back to the Super Bowl again.

Once we got our players healthy and the players knew the system and we were playing together, we developed a bond. We were a team in the truest sense of the word. We cared about each other. We rooted for each other. We thought that if everybody did his job the best he could, we could reach this point. That's what Bill and all of the coaches kept telling us.

When we were 0–2 and 1–3, we didn't panic. We stuck to our guns. We knew it was a long season and there would be some ups and downs. Our down time just happened to come at the beginning of the season. But we learned a lot from 1996 when we started 0–2 and went to the Super Bowl.

It was awful what happened to Drew [Bledsoe], a man I truly admire and respect. We came up together in 1993. He was the first-round pick; I was the eighth rounder. We started at different ends of the spectrum, but we played together for nine years. We have a bond, a friendship that we'll have forever. It was so special to see Drew come into the AFC championship game in Pittsburgh and pick us up like that. I'm happy he got to experience a part of the season like that.

For Tom Brady to step in for Drew, providing us with leadership and distributing the ball as he did, was unbelievable. We had confidence in Tom even in preseason, and I knew how hard he worked in the off-season conditioning program to get his body bulked up and to really learn our offensive system. All that preparation paid off.

We had players who stepped up every week, such as Antowain Smith, David Patten, Ty Law, Lawyer Milloy, Anthony Pleasant, Roman Phifer, Bryan Cox, Ted Johnson, Willie McGinest, Tedy

Bruschi, Otis Smith, Tebucky Jones, Mike Vrabel, Bobby Hamilton; and our entire offensive line—Damien Woody, Mike Compton, Joe Andruzzi, Greg Robinson-Randall, Matt Light, Grey Ruegamer, Grant Williams—was unbelievable. Guys like Kevin Faulk, Patrick Pass, Marc Edwards, Fred Coleman, Charles Johnson, J. R. Redmond, Jermaine Wiggins, Rod Rutledge, Matt Stevens, Lonie Paxton, Antwan Harris, Terrell Buckley, Terrance Shaw, Je'Rod Cherry, Damon Huard, Brandon Mitchell, Dave Nugent, Chris Sullivan, Terry Glenn, Leonard Myers, Matt Chatham, Riddick Parker, Kenyatta Jones, Larry Izzo, Arther Love, Jabari Holloway, Adrian Klemm, Drew Inzer, Kole Ayi, Stephen Neal, and Jace Sayler all played their roles.

We had a great kicker in Adam Vinatieri, who made the most unbelievable kicks at the most pressure-filled moments. We had a talented punter in Ken Walter, who had such great hang time it was tough for the other team to ever have good field position.

We really believed that our special teams could make a difference in winning and losing. Coach [Brad] Seely did a great job.

I don't want to leave anybody out because all 53 men on this team and the guys who helped prepare us every week on the practice squad need to take part of the credit for this. We had coaches who worked all day and night. Our trainers, our equipment people, our front office, our owner.

I had never seen anything come together like this.

As a team we knew it was happening. It took the rest of the world a little more time, but I think our fans knew it too, just by the way they supported us even in the bad times. It's been a great experience for me. I go out and people want to see my ring, and they're disappointed when I tell them I haven't got it yet. But I'll be wearing it on my finger proudly for years to come. I feel so good for the people who waited 42 years for this. The fans deserved this.

But I lost some respect for some people around football who didn't believe we were worthy of winning a Super Bowl. I sometimes wonder how that could have come out of their mouths. People were saying that just because there weren't a lot of balls being thrown down the field, it wasn't a great Super Bowl. The state of football as it is, you just don't score a lot of offensive touchdowns.

It was a great Super Bowl. I'll never forget it. Our fans will never forget it, and most of football will never forget it. They'll never forget how much we gave every time we stepped on the field. How hard we tried to win every game. How much preparation we needed to have to take on every opponent and get the upper hand on every matchup we had on the field. This is what football was all about. It was about being together as a team, implementing the game plans, believing in ourselves. It was about never giving in to anybody. And when the chance came in every game to win it, we did it. It was an amazing ride.

I'll be able to show and tell my kids what their old man did.

Thank you all for being a part of it with us.

—Troy Brown
March 27, 2002

Acknowledgments

I wish to thank my wife, Leeanne; my son, Ben; and my daughter, Emilee, for their constant support and love and for allowing me to devote so much time to this project. Thanks to my parents, Nicola and Adelina Cafardo, and my brother, Fred, for all they've done for me. Thanks to Barbara Wood, a special mother-in-law.

Thanks to Bill Belichick, Scott Pioli, Robert and Jonathan Kraft, Drew Henson, Troy Brown, Adam Vinatieri, Eddie Andelman, Steve Burton, Terry Glenn, and Jon Gruden for their contributions.

Thanks to the Patriots' PR department: Stacey James, Kathleen Whiteside, Anthony Moretti, and Berj Najarian for their help. Also thanks to Barbara Rizzo.

I wish to thank Tom Bast, Blythe Hurley, and Bilal Dardai of Triumph Books for their hard work in putting the book together.

Special thanks to Globies Don Skwar, Joe Sullivan, Reid Laymance, Ron Borges, Michael Smith, and the entire staff of writers and editors who took part in coverage of the 2001 season.

Special thanks to Chris Kennedy, Ken Powers, Alan Greenberg, Dan Pires, and Sean McDonough for their friendship. A special pat on the back for Ron Hobson of the *Patriot Ledger*, a former colleague, who spent 42 years watching the Patriots and, as fate would have it, covered a championship team for the first time before retiring.

CHAPTER 1

The Impossible Moment

After eight consecutive sub-.500 seasons, including a second straight ninth-place finish in the American League in 1966, Red Sox general manager Dick O'Connell decided to place his faith in the young, brash, and confident Dick Williams, who had successfully managed his Triple-A affiliate in Toronto. After accepting the job, Williams was asked how he thought the team would do in the upcoming 1967 season. He predicted, "We'll win more than we lose."

Beating 100 to 1 odds to win the American League pennant with a team of young players and two budding superstars in Carl Yastrzemski, who won the MVP and the Triple Crown, and Jim Lonborg, who won the Cy Young Award, the team became known as the "Impossible Dream" Red Sox. Unfortunately, they fell one game short of a World Series championship, losing Game 7, 7–2, to the St. Louis Cardinals.

In a different era and a different sport, but part of the same starving-for-a-championship fan base, New England Patriots head coach Bill Belichick, off a 5–11 last-place season in the American Football Conference East division in 2000, said of his team's chances in 2001, "We'll be more competitive. We'll have more depth."

On the evening of February 3, 2002, at the Superdome in New Orleans in a suspended second or two, kicker Adam Vinatieri proceeded toward the ball with short, swift steps, driving it with the full force of his right leg, creating a perfect follow-through that sent the ball end-over-end 48 yards through the uprights and into all time. Vinatieri extended his arms in triumph.

The Patriots—the "Impossible Team"—had paid back St. Louis for an entire generation of frustrated Boston sports fans, beating the 14-point favorite St. Louis Rams in Super Bowl XXXVI, 20–17.

Boston sports teams have certainly had a thing about meeting teams from St. Louis in the finals. In 1970 the NHL's Boston Bruins defeated the St. Louis Blues in four straight games to win the Stanley Cup. Those of us old enough to remember will never forget Bobby Orr's overtime goal to beat the Blues on May 10, 1970, as he went flying through the air in a photo frozen in our minds. And we will never forget Boston shortstop Rico Petrocelli catching the final out of the final regular-season game in 1967 and jumping for joy while sending a Fenway Park crowd into disbelief. Just as we will never forget a Patriots team crashing from the sideline toward the middle of the field, embracing Vinatieri amid the sparkle of flashbulbs combined with a shower of red, white, and blue confetti, creating a fireworks effect without the explosives.

We understand that the greatest upset in Super Bowl history was the 18-point underdog New York Jets clipping the Baltimore Colts in Super Bowl III. But was New England–St. Louis not one of the greatest Super Bowl games?

The Patriots and their fans thought so.

* * *

In the higher elevations of the Superdome, owner Bob Kraft had been keeping his wife Myra's hand over his heart during the final moments of the game. When it was over he leaped and embraced son Jonathan, as several moments of the most intense and heartfelt emotion the sport has ever known were under way.

Kraft, a Patriots season-ticket holder since 1971, had been a long-time Boston sports fan, dabbling in sports ownership with the Boston Lobsters of World Team Tennis. In 1983 he purchased Foxboro Stadium but waited patiently for the opportunity to own the entire team. That opportunity came in 1994, one year after the franchise had been jump-started with the hiring of coach Bill Parcells and the drafting of Washington State University quarterback Drew Bledsoe as the first overall pick in the draft.

In eight short years of ownership, Kraft has already presided over two Super Bowl teams and five playoff teams. But now he is the owner of the World Champion New England Patriots, the first in the franchise's 42-year history. The Vince Lombardi Trophy has a resting place in New England forever.

"The league people had come to my box with a few minutes left to take me downstairs to the ceremony, but I told them, 'I'm not going anywhere until this is over.' If we won, I thought they couldn't start the ceremony without me anyway. So I stayed until Adam made the field goal, and then I went down. I had to stay and watch it. I couldn't risk being en route somewhere and missing the greatest sports moment of my life," said Kraft.

It's true. This wasn't just any moment. This was a memory chiseled in the brain for a lifetime. The only thing better would have been if the game had been played in Foxboro, Massachusetts, where New England fans could have witnessed it firsthand.

We had seen the "We Are Family" Pittsburgh Pirates in the seventies, but these were truly the "We Are Team" New England Patriots.

"Absolutely incredible," said a teary-eyed quarterback Tom Brady, who was the Super Bowl MVP after leading the Patriots on the final drive to set up Vinatieri's winning kick. "This is what happens when guys believe in each other. And there's so many reasons why we're here."

They believed in each other because of players like All-Pro safety Lawyer Milloy, who demanded the world take notice. The defensive cocaptain and team leader, Milloy spoke out against anyone who disrespected them. No surprise that he was the first to give Belichick a bear hug, lift him off the ground, and lug him around like a rag doll. It is not known whether Belichick's ribs survived the jubilation, but at the very least the coach felt the love.

Mouths and eyes were wide open. Fingers were pointing to the heavens. Veteran guard Mike Compton, a WWF Steve Austin lookalike, plopped his body facedown on the field. Tedy Bruschi did the same closer to midfield. Brady, a kid at heart but with a major-league arm, will be forever visualized pounding on Bledsoe's shoulders and screaming, "We won!"

Hearts raced as the historic significance of the evening turned screams and cheers to tears. From the players to the coaches, from the owner to the fans watching at the Superdome, and from bars in Copley Square in Boston to the "End Zone" in Foxboro, people were watching—almost 1.3 million viewers, the most-watched program in Boston television history.

"God's hand was at work here," insisted Kraft.

Who could argue?

It was a season that came right out of the pages of *Mission Impossible*. The Patriots had 70-1 odds to win the Super Bowl at the start of the season and were 14-point underdogs that fateful day. Las Vegas lost its shirt on the Patriots, but New England won a warm overcoat to keep it fuzzy and toasty for years to come.

"Now do you think we'll start getting some good publicity?" asked Patriots center Damien Woody, who was one of the players who carried the "no respect" theme.

In actuality the team received growing respect each week of its season after it had beaten the New Orleans Saints on November 25, which began a nine-game winning streak to the title. But it was a team mantra—us versus them—and it worked famously.

It is true that the players often told the media that they were better than we thought. When they spoke to us in terms of team and focus we shrugged it off as sports cliché. When they said they feared no team, we thought they were a little cocky, perhaps overconfident. When they were 1–3 and the season appeared lost, they kept saying, "Hold on just a minute, give us a chance."

"It just felt right," said veteran cornerback Terrell Buckley. "It felt right from the start. There was something, that . . . well, you just can't put your hands on, that was right. And even though we struggled, you know, we knew at some point we wouldn't."

After losing to the Rams, 24–17, on November 18, a week before Thanksgiving, they never lost again.

They won exciting, hard-fought games. They won ugly games.

Brady went from fourth-string quarterback in 2000 after he was taken in the sixth round out of Michigan to superstar before our eyes, taking the place of the established Bledsoe, who went down with massive internal injuries following a jarring sideline hit by New York Jets linebacker Mo Lewis on September 23. Brady was voted to the Pro Bowl. He was the Super Bowl MVP, at age 24 the youngest to ever win the honor.

Troy Brown, who had caught a team-record 101 passes in the regular season, was finally recognized as one of the top playmakers in the game. Milloy took Ray Lewis' spot as the toughest SOB in the business. Ty Law rejuvenated his career and became a big-play cornerback once again. Antowain Smith gave the Patriots a legitimate running game. Otis Smith, the oldest starting cornerback in the NFL, proved he was far from washed up. The offensive line was the best since 1996.

They won games early and late. They won in bad weather and in good weather, inside and outside, grass and turf. They won with great special teams, a kicker with ice water in his veins.

"They blocked great up front; the snap and the hold was great. Once I kicked it, I knew it was good. I looked up and it was time to celebrate," said Vinatieri.

"We thought before the game he had 55-yard range," said Patriots offensive coordinator Charlie Weis. "That guy has been unbelievable."

They won with great coaching.

No team was tougher.

"It was force versus finesse and something had to give," said nitty-gritty linebacker Tedy Bruschi. "It wasn't too complicated: we just concentrated on hitting them hard."

When Rams quarterback Kurt Warner took his jersey off after the game, his chest and stomach were bruised. When receiver Isaac Bruce had a chance to breathe after the loss, he realized he couldn't inhale very well because he had broken his ribs on a Ty Law hit earlier in the game.

They all felt like champions. Brady was going to Disney World. The team went straight to the Wheaties Box cover.

"I feel like Rocky tonight," said Bruschi. There were 45 Rockys on the field that night.

* * *

The Patriots offense struggled mightily in the first half. They needed a big play. They needed to capitalize on a mistake. The defense, so strong and determined that night, obliged.

Warner dropped back to throw with 8:49 remaining in the second quarter, but all he saw was linebacker Mike Vrabel closing in. Vrabel had easily faked substitute right tackle Rod Jones, playing with a strained right groin in place of the injured Ryan Tucker. Vrabel hit Warner in the head and got away with it, redirecting the throw intended for Bruce. The ball was picked off by Law, who ran it 47 yards to the end zone, giving the Patriots a 7–3 lead.

"I never saw Vrabel, but I knew we were going to pressure him [Warner]. I was just out there waiting for the play to unfold, so to speak, and the ball just came my way and I took it in," said Law.

On the other side of the two-minute warning, Warner completed a slant to Rams receiver Rickey Proehl, who had the ball stripped by Antwan Harris on a nice play not far from the surface.

The ball squirted loose and Buckley, who returned it to the Rams' 40, recovered it.

The Patriots offense clicked just in time.

Tom Brady hit Troy Brown on an inside route for 16 yards to the 24. He connected with Jermaine Wiggins for nine yards, pitched to Kevin Faulk for seven down the left sideline, and then tossed a soft pass over Dexter McLeon's reach into the hands of David Patten, who made a circus catch and held on for six more points with 31 seconds remaining.

The Patriots walked away with a shocking 14–3 halftime lead.

No team had ever overcome a deficit of 10 or more points at halftime in the Super Bowl.

The Patriots were pretty "pumped and jacked" in the immortal words of their former coach Pete Carroll, but some of the veteran players were trying desperately to contain the enthusiasm, getting in the faces of those who were a little overconfident halfway through the most important game of their lives.

Just as the Rams appeared to be getting into a rhythm midway through the third quarter, Otis Smith picked off a Warner pass after Torry Holt fell down. Smith then ran it back 30 yards, setting up Vinatieri's 37-yard field goal to give the Patriots a 17–3 lead.

The Patriots played the second half as they had hoped they would the first half, utilizing Antowain Smith (92 yards), who battled through tender moments with an ailing right leg to control the ball on offense with timely runs that ate serious time off the second-half clock.

"I spent some time on the bench just getting retaped, just trying to get the right feel," said Smith.

The Patriots were simply remarkable on defense at this point. Defensive coordinator Romeo Crennel, who sometimes was overshadowed by Belichick's defensive genius, had an outstanding plan coming into the game. He wanted the Patriots to keep Marshall Faulk from getting to the outside. He wanted to saturate Warner's weapons, often using six and even seven defensive backs, and he wanted his players to be really physical with the Rams receivers.

All of these tactics eventually worked in wearing down the Rams, holding Faulk to 130 yards—76 rushing, 54 receiving—and leaving Rams fans wondering why Faulk didn't handle the ball more.

But there were moments of angst and doubt. Well, maybe no doubt by the team, but Patriots fans, who were watching intently at neighborhood drinking holes and in their living rooms in the New England area, had to wonder, was this too good to be true?

What would happen to destroy this moment?

Don't think it didn't cross my mind, either. After all, I was at Shea Stadium for Game 6 of the World Series in 1986 when the Red Sox had the Mets beat, and a horrified Red Sox Nation watched a series of events unfold, including the ball going through Bill Buckner's legs, to destroy what would have been the greatest sports moment ever in New England.

Who didn't compare veteran pass rusher Willie McGinest to Buckner when with just 10 minutes remaining he was called for holding Faulk? Tebucky Jones had scooped up a Warner fumble and scampered 96 yards on a bum leg for a touchdown that didn't count.

Kraft remembers thinking, along with the rest of us: "Bill Buckner."

"I'm not the referee so I don't know if it was holding or not," said McGinest. "I played him the same way all game. It was disappointing at the time, but my teammates told me to forget about it and go to the next play."

It could be said that if McGinest didn't hold Faulk, the best all-around player in the league might have got free and caught a pass from Warner for a touchdown. McGinest had done a superb job spying Faulk and keeping the ball away from him.

Yet, after the holding call the Rams got the ball at the 1 and a first down. Two plays later Warner went in on a one-yard keeper with 9:31 left. The Rams had pulled to within one touchdown.

The Patriots went from a potential 24–3 lead to a 17–10 lead.

Fired up, the Rams defense smothered the Patriots on the next series as pass rusher Leonard Little, who hadn't been heard from too often, hurried Brady into a bad throw and fourth down.

McGinest redeemed himself with about four minutes to go when he sacked Warner for a 16-yard loss after the Rams had driven to the Patriots '39. It created a third-and-25, but after a penalty on Seymour for offside, Warner couldn't hit Holt down the field. The Rams chose to punt instead of going for it at the 45 on fourth down with less than four minutes to go.

"It felt good because it took them out of field goal range," said McGinest.

But the Rams finally tied it 17–17 with 1:30 remaining when Warner connected with Proehl on a 26-yard touchdown pass on a play where Proehl caught the ball and then put a nifty fake on Jones and Terrance Shaw.

Charlie Weis' play chart had one very poignant sentence written in black ink on the top of the chart: "Take Care of the Ball. No Turnovers."

"How many did we have? That's right. None," said Weis afterward.

Weis said he and Bill Belichick had a "30-second conversation" during a timeout on the sideline following the Rams' tying score, which led to an 81-second drive to infamy.

"Let's win it right here," said Weis.

Weis knew so many others wanted them to take a knee and head into overtime. One of them was Fox commentator John Madden, who soon ate his words.

"They had the momentum and we had to stop their momentum and win the game," said Weis. "We needed to play to win."

The Patriots may have run a conservative offense through most of the season to protect young Brady, but there was nothing conservative about the way they approached the final drive.

"Sling it," was the advice Bledsoe gave to his young understudy Brady. "Go out there and win the game. It's what legends are made of."

Brady was an efficient but not spectacular 16 for 27 for 145 yards, one touchdown, and no interceptions. He had no timeouts remaining when the Patriots started their final drive.

The Patriots pulled out all the stops at this point. As Weis pointed out, the momentum had shifted. Belichick had Troy Brown receive the kickoff. Brown had not been used in this capacity all season. But earlier in the week it was rumored that the team might go to Brown in a key situation.

This was it.

The Rams, however, did a good job of containing Brown and stopped him at the 17.

This is where young Brady had to start what would be the winning drive with, let us repeat, 1:21 remaining and no timeouts.

Brady was 24 but he acted like he was 34. Calm. Cool. He responded as if he'd done this before. Maybe he had been there in his dreams. But he knew what to do.

"That minute-and-30-second drive has got to be one of the biggest drives in Super Bowl history," said Bruschi.

In seven plays, Brady moved the team from the 17 to the Rams' 30.

"Tom did a super job of managing the game," Belichick said of his quarterback.

He threw five yards to J. R. Redmond, eight yards to Redmond, eleven yards to Redmond.

The key play was a 23-yard pass to Brown. A short pass to Wiggins put the ball on the 30 and set the stage for Vinatieri.

"That was the big play," Brady said. "It's called '64 Max All-End,' and the *Max* stands for, as my coach says, 'We need the maximum time for me to throw.'"

Brown caught it around his chin area and promptly ran to the sideline.

"The way the Rams play, they really read the quarterback's eyes," explained Brady. "I was looking hard to the right, and Troy [Brown] slipped behind them. They lost sight of him. I hit him and he did the rest."

With the ball resting at the 36, the Patriots needed more. Brady tossed to Wiggins for six yards to the 30. That's where he patiently lined the team up, did the normal snap count, and spiked the ball.

"What Tom Brady just did gives me goose bumps," said Madden, a good comeback line to his earlier comment.

Now the odds were unbelievably in New England's favor. Vinatieri had never missed in 23 attempts indoors in his pro career.

"Shoot," said Antowain Smith, "after he kicked one through the snow, I knew he could kick one through the confetti."

Said Vinatieri, "I was just so happy that the guys moved the ball down and gave me an opportunity. Once I kicked it, I knew it was good. I looked up and it was just time to celebrate. It was unbelievable."

*   *   *

This sportswriter sat motionless in his seat in the press box at the Superdome in New Orleans, as the field area was a sky of confetti and players were leaping onto the field and into each other's arms.

Quickly, with an NFL type hovering over my shoulder, waiting for the MVP ballot I was contemplating, I had to make the tough decision on who would be the game MVP. After all, what I had witnessed through 16 games and an equally improbable postseason was the epitome of the word *team*.

In 21 years of writing about the Red Sox and the Patriots, I had never witnessed a group of athletes other than the final Boston Celtics banner winners in 1986 so in tune with themselves, their coach, and their desire to win it all. I had never seen a group of athletes be so inspired and steadfast in proving to the majority of prognosticators who didn't give them a chance of being .500 for the season, let alone winning a Super Bowl, that they were for real. In pursuit of respect, they won a Super Bowl.

So how could there be one MVP?

The *Providence Journal*'s Jim Donaldson thought the MVP would have fittingly gone to the *team*, not one individual. After all, this was the team that came out together during the Super Bowl introductions and set the tone for the entire game before it even started.

Donaldson was right—the entire *team* should have been voted MVP, but with a gun to my head I went with Vinatieri, who made the biggest pressure kick of all time and who just three weeks earlier, in Foxboro, had made the most memorable kick perhaps of all time in the divisional playoffs—a 45-yarder through a snowstorm to upset the Oakland Raiders.

Brady, who led the team down the field in the final 1:21 for the final kick, ultimately got the nod as Internet voters, who received 4 of the 19 votes, put him over the top in close voting among Brady, Ty Law, and Adam Vinatieri.

Brady said afterward that the 2002 Cadillac Escalade would be shared with his teammates.

And you'd have to believe him on that.

*　*　*

If you know much about Patriots history, you understand the magnitude of the feat. It had taken 42 years, granted, a mere half the time since the Red Sox had won the World Series (1918), but when you asked the general sports fan which of Boston's major teams would win a championship first, the Patriots didn't slip off the tongue.

In fact, prior to their championship they had gone the longest of any of the four major sports—baseball, football, hockey, and basketball—among franchises that began during the JFK years without winning a championship.

For the most part, this was a franchise with a sad history since entering the AFL in 1960. The Patriots got to the AFL championship in 1963 but lost 51–10 to the San Diego Chargers. They were in two Super Bowls, in 1986 and 1997, but lost to the Chicago Bears and the Green Bay Packers, respectively. Outstanding coaches like Chuck Fairbanks, Raymond Berry, and Bill Parcells couldn't win the brass ring.

This was a team that once called out Bob Gladieux's name over the intercom at Harvard Stadium because one of their players, John Charles, had failed to sign a contract in time for the game. There were great years under Fairbanks in the seventies, but a Ben Dreith call on Ray "Sugar Bear" Hamilton had led to a loss in the playoffs against Oakland. That was considered the greatest Patriots team of all time until this one, but their quest was cut short because of that infamous call.

The Patriots went to the Super Bowl in 1986 and were crushed by the Bears. After some low years in the nineties, Parcells rejuiced the Patriots and got them to Super Bowl XXX, only to lose to the Packers, 35–21. A few days later, Parcells quit as Patriots head coach.

The Patriots headed a select group, all right.

The Minnesota Vikings, for instance, have gone championshipless since they played their first NFL game in September 1961. They won the NFL championship in 1969, but they lost to AFL champion Kansas City that year in Super Bowl IV.

The Los Angeles/California/Anaheim Angels have played in Southern California since 1961, and the closest they ever got to a World Series was against the Red Sox in the 1986 American League championship game, while the 1961 Washington Senators/Texas Rangers have also fallen well short. The Houston Colt 45s and Houston Astros have been around since 1962 with nothing to show for it. They now have the same albatross the Patriots carried for so long.

Kraft was more aware of the lean years than anyone. Throughout the amazing journey, Kraft had great confidence that this was indeed a team of destiny. He would often visit the team before they played, and he always walked away with the feeling they knew they could win.

That was the sense that night.

During player introductions before the game, the players decided to come out as a team rather than be introduced individually, sending a message to the Rams right off the bat that they were a united group and it would be very hard to break their resolve.

"When I walked out of there [the locker room], I knew we were going to win the game," said Kraft. "I could just feel it in the locker room. Bill was calm. The players were calm. They had that look."

That "look" was built from the ground up months before.

CHAPTER 2

This Is Tougher than Legos

Until director of player personnel Scott Pioli put together a Super Bowl team, he was known more as Bill Parcells' son-in-law than a budding genius and a great judge of talent. Even after he'd signed 21 low-priced free agents, nobody was wowed.

Not at the time, anyway.

As it turned out, he should have been the Executive of the Year, hitting on so many players who played key roles with the 2001 Patriots.

Anthony Pleasant, Roman Phifer, Bryan Cox, and Terrell Buckley didn't make Patriots fans faint with excitement. Mike Vrabel had never started a game in three years with the Steelers. Larry Izzo was a Pro Bowl special teamer, but why didn't the Dolphins want him back? The Philadelphia Eagles rejected Charles Johnson and Torrance Small. David Patten was a journeyman receiver, third or fourth on the depth chart. Antowain Smith, a former No. 1 pick, was wondering if anyone would give him a job after the Buffalo Bills dumped him after two years of burying him on the roster. Mike Compton had been a starter, but what—suddenly the Detroit Lions didn't think he could play? Fullback Marc Edwards barely played in Cleveland.

What was the allure?

What reason would anyone have for thinking the 2001 Patriots would be the crème de la crème other than blind love of the home team?

Belichick and Pioli kept speaking about depth and how the Patriots suddenly had more of it. Even that was a hard sell following a 5–11 season.

Pioli said he was looking for football players—players who put football first in their lives. He wasn't looking at stopwatches but at players who played football speed. At that time it was an interesting concept, but it sounded too simple. Didn't all football players put football first? Well, not exactly. Pioli was on to something.

When he was learning the business in Cleveland and then in Baltimore and New York, he envisioned being in a position to shape a team. He and Cleveland Indians general manager Mark Shapiro, an administrative assistant with the Indians in the early nineties, the same time Pioli was an assistant with the Browns, often spoke about how character and teamwork could mold a team.

This was Pioli's chance. What did he do with it? He shaped a Super Bowl team.

* * *

On March 7, Drew Bledsoe signed a 10-year, $103 million deal, ending speculation that he might be traded. If the Patriots knew then about Brady what they knew a few months later, Bledsoe probably wouldn't have been signed.

So the prognosticators made their preseason predictions. The most popular record prediction echoed in the media was 7–9, slightly better than the disaster of 2000. It at least showed progress, and that was what Kraft needed as he moved the team into the

$325 million privately financed state-of-the-art CMGI Field in 2002. He needed to show *something* if he was going to justify higher ticket prices.

The Patriots had gone the bargain-basement approach the year before. But Raymont Harris, Eric Bjornson, Chris Calloway, Jon Harris, Chad Cascadden, and others who came through the doors in 2000 later had to be careful not to get hit on the backside on their way out the door.

Bjornson was cast as the player who could replace Ben Coates. But early on the *Boston Globe*'s Ron Borges made this observation: "*Bjornson* is Swedish for no hands." Bjornson was cut during the 2000 season.

There were successes. Belichick and Pioli brought in Bobby Hamilton, a defensive end from the Jets who had been buried in Parcells' doghouse. But Belichick, the defensive coordinator with the Jets, never agreed with Parcells' assessment of Hamilton, and the affable backup, grateful to have his career salvaged, became the starter, a role he has yet to give up.

The philosophy Belichick had agreed to when he took the job as head coach had been written by Patriots chief operating officer Andy Wasynczuk, who had come to understand that the Patriots needed to build with not only good players but also ones who fit the financial scheme in place.

It was Wasynczuk who had taken the heat for losing Curtis Martin a few years back, failing to tie him up long-term before the Jets swooped in with a killer offer the team could not match. But big contracts to Max Lane, Todd Rucci, Willie McGinest, and Ted Johnson hadn't yielded bang for their buck.

The Patriots decided to change their ways.

Wasynczuk's economic staff—business/contract negotiator Jack Mula and researcher and player compensation analyst Richard Miller—should receive as many accolades for their research and ability to spot trends as Belichick and Pioli do for their ability to tap the right free agents. By knowing the salary cap situation of every team in the league, Wasynczuk was able to determine which players might become free through teams having to cut payroll. If there was a "patient" approach to Belichick and Pioli's procurement of free agents, it was through the information Wasynczuk provided them. This was especially true when it came to late signings, such as Cox, Phifer, Smith, and Buckley.

"Credit Bill [Belichick] and Scott [Pioli] with finding the players," Wasynczuk said. "Unless you're finding good players who make a difference, it doesn't matter how good a contract you do. We've all been on the same page. They've found talented guys. In the last year and a half, we've had to restock. The same constraints that have hit other teams . . . we knew we were heading that way if we didn't change the way we did our business. We're sitting in a pretty good state right now."

Wasynczuk has also convinced veterans to take minimum salaries with moderate incentives to reach desirable salary levels.

Play for pay. What a concept. Too bad the other major sports can't implement this.

Antowain Smith provided a good example. Wasynczuk and Mula signed Smith to a one-year deal for $477,000 with a $25,000 signing bonus, small potatoes for a former No. 1 draft pick. But in his comeback season, Smith wound up earning over $1 million because of performance and playtime incentives.

"Antowain earned more with the Patriots than he was scheduled to earn with the Bills when they cut him," said Smith's agent, Kennard McGuire.

Wasynczuk said, "A big part of what we're building is consistency of philosophy. What's critical is for Bill or Scott and myself, in assessing the economics, we have to be 100 percent on the same page. When there are differences—and I've experienced that too—the product will fall short. It's been great with Bill and Scott on communication. There's a good understanding how that player will fill in, what role they'll have. Whether it's Jack [Mula] or myself, we'll put a proposal together and work through it with the agent, a package to secure the player's services for the season or for a couple of seasons while making sure it works well for us as an organization.

"Sometimes a contract gets set up with incentives, but sometimes if you set it up for, say, interceptions, well, that takes the place of a coach. You don't want your contract being the coach. You want your coach being the coach. We've been very careful in the kind of incentives built into the contract. . . . You want it to be grouped with team performance, and at the same time, you want some individual aspect accounted for."

The Patriots won the Super Bowl with the third lowest payroll in football, a formula other NFL teams would surely copy.

"The nature of sports is if something works, or perceives to work, copy or emulate it until the next thing comes up, and see what the next successful program is doing. Back six or seven years ago, teams were getting creative by pushing salary cap moneys into the future; it hurt a lot of people. You have to be careful of the lemming philosophy: just because everyone else is doing it we should do it. In the end you have to break it down, developing a philosophy that works for your team," explained Wasynczuk.

Wasynczuk also changed the way he did business with draft choices. After resistance from the union and some agents over incentive-filled deals, Wasynczuk and Mula proved they weren't out to pull the wool over their eyes.

Mula, who has very successfully executed the philosophy of the organization, is unique in that he has been a player agent (Doug Flutie, Qadry Ismail, and Priest Holmes are among his former clients) and now is negotiating on the other side.

In the case of Richard Seymour, the sixth overall pick, the way Wasynczuk and Mula wound up structuring the contract, the Patriots' inclusion of incentives rewards Seymour over the length of the contract if he becomes one of the top players at his position. The Patriots were one of the few teams that got their high draft pick in camp on time.

Even with Brady two years ago, the Patriots wound up getting him signed for a signing bonus $10,000 less than market value, but the Patriots placed some playing incentives in the deal. Brady earned $70,000 more than his minimum salary because of the playtime incentives he earned.

"Any time you're trying to work on a deal you try to get protection," said Wasynczuk. "Players are looking for fair compensation and to establish stability for themselves. One thing our sport is well positioned on is we don't have guaranteed contracts. It hurts the other sports in getting players to play at their highest ability game in and game out. We try to avoid turning it into a guaranteed contract."

Practicing frugal economics meant making tough decisions. Older players, such as Larry Whigham, offensive tackle Bruce Armstrong, defensive tackle Henry Thomas, and linebacker Chris Slade, were let loose.

Armstrong, a six-time Pro Bowler, had wanted to play at least another year, and perhaps a year in CMGI. But it wasn't to be. Despite starting 16 games in 2000, the Patriots coaching staff thought it best to begin finding a younger left tackle, at the time hoping Adrian Klemm, the second-round pick in the 2000 draft and the first pick of the Belichick era, would take the job, but he did not.

The Patriots had hoped to bring back Thomas, a sage vet who really helped out the younger defensive linemen, but he was unwilling to take a big salary cut to stay with the team. He and the Patriots parted. As it turned out, Anthony Pleasant took on Thomas' role.

The Patriots lost popular nose tackle Chad Eaton in free agency. The free-spirited Eaton had demanded a market deal to stay in New England, but the Patriots had a number in mind for Eaton, and his agent, Gary Uberstine, far exceeded it. The Patriots got all of their free agents signed to signing bonuses totaling $2.7 million, while Eaton cost the Seahawks a $3.5 million bonus. This one move came to symbolize the direction the Patriots were taking. They were in control of their payroll. No agent or player was going to hold them up.

Eaton: "There was a price I had and they weren't willing to go there, but there are no hard feelings. I understood. And it worked out great for me because I live here [Seattle] anyway. My family is here, my wife's family is here, and now we're all together as a family. And we're building toward something here, too. We came very close to putting it together and making the playoffs and I think there's hope we'll get there next season."

Thomas retired. Eaton went home to Seattle. Whigham again found Pro Bowl status in Chicago. Slade went to the hapless Panthers.

Thomas, who really helped starting defensive tackle Brandon Mitchell refocus on his career, said of Mitchell's performance in 2001, "I'm proud that Brandon recommitted his life to being a better football player and being what he was supposed to be when the Patriots first drafted him. It's really a tribute to him. I talked to him a lot in the off-season and early in the season, and hopefully I helped him a little bit. But he's done things on his own."

It was bittersweet for Whigham. He never wanted to leave the Patriots, but his salary was rising too high. The Patriots replaced him with Larry Izzo, and things worked out well for both players.

The Patriots also had some interesting moves that were never consummated. They made Pittsburgh Steelers running back Chris Fuamatu-Ma'afala, a 5'11", 250-pound horse, a one-year $700,000 offer. But the Steelers matched it and retained him. That's when the Patriots decided to sign Antowain Smith, a free agent who had been dumped by the Bills; Smith ran for 1,157 yards and 12 touchdowns for the Patriots. Not getting "Fu" was the best move the Patriots never made.

Similarly, the Patriots were also trying to move on quarterback Ray Lucas, who had played for Belichick and Weis in New York. Lucas had been with the Patriots in 1996 as a practice-squad receiver, but he moved with Belichick and Bill Parcells to New York. The irony there is that a snowstorm canceled a trip to New England. While waiting to reschedule it, Lucas visited Miami and signed.

The Patriots turned around and inked Dolphins' reject Damon Huard, who wound up losing his No. 2 job to Brady. But Huard was a huge factor in the quarterback troika. According to Weis, he was used as a sounding board and kept things sane when Bledsoe was going through pangs of not being able to get his starting job back.

The Patriots were certainly a revolving door for a while. Marty Moore, Torrance Small, Lee Johnson, Sean Morey, Marc Megna, Rob Gatrell, Larry Bowie, Shockmain Davis, Chris Eitzmann, and Bert Emanuel were a part of the team at one time. Also around and about were Tony George, Reggie Grimes, Ray Hill, Rob Holmberg, Curtis Jackson, Garrett Johnson, Adrian Klemm, Dane Looker, Johnny McWilliams, Chuck Osborne, Jeff Paulk, Kato Serwanga, Tony Simmons, Greg Spires, Owen Pochman, T. J. Turner, Terrance Beadles, Brad Costello, Antico Dalton, Ronney Daniels, Adam Davis, Dan Hadenfeldt, Maggie Tuitele, Josh Rawlings, and Yubrenal Isabelle.

Little by little, the team began taking shape. The strength program, headed by Mike Woicick, had some of the most successful results. Brady benefited most, gaining some 20 pounds of muscle. "It was not only the physical part, but he was improving in the passing camps and minicamps," said Belichick.

In early April, the Patriots signed Compton and Patten. It didn't shake the New England region, but both players added so much. Compton gave the Patriots toughness on the line they hadn't had. And Patten became a deep threat, essentially replacing Shawn Jefferson after he signed a lucrative free-agent deal with Atlanta in 2000.

*　*　*

A no-tolerance approach when it came to foolishness had permeated through the Patriots front office, ownership, and coach. After a 5–11 season in 2001, Kraft was taking a tough approach.

During Super Bowl XXXV in Tampa, Kraft was furious when Ty Law was caught with the illegal drug Ecstasy at the Canadian border on December 18, 1999, the morning after a big Patriots win over

Buffalo. Law and two other Patriots, wide receivers Terry Glenn and Troy Brown, had stayed behind to avoid flying in a blizzard. (All three players are afraid to fly.)

Richard Berthelsen, the general counsel of the NFL Players' Association, found the Patriots' punishment of Law—a suspension without pay, which amounted to a one-game paycheck of $87,500—"excessive." But Kraft was going after much more. Even though Law claimed he had grabbed the wrong duffel bag, one belonging to a cousin, before leaving his home for the trip, Kraft was going after about $10 million of Law's $14.2 million signing bonus.

Kraft said at a breakfast with the media, owners have to be "vigilant in this area. From my point of view, anyone who acts inappropriately, I'd like to see us be able to recapture his signing bonus and redistribute it to the players, so you're not just penalizing that individual player and saving money under the cap. We'd be obligated to spend it. The reason 105–110 million watch our games from Sunday to Monday is the quality of product on the field. I think it's a huge negative if they see a stream of people who aren't worthy."

Kraft applied that tough stance toward Glenn's bonus when he violated the NFL's drug policy.

The Law situation had a happy ending, as Law's agents dropped their grievance against the Patriots pursuing the game check of $87,500. Kraft got together with Law and the two of them worked out a program at the Dana Farber Cancer Institute in Boston, which helps in blood platelet donations.

As strange as it sounds, the Law incident also was the first sign of team togetherness. Both Brown and Glenn had risked missing the meetings the next day because they didn't want to leave their teammate behind. So they waited for him and returned to Boston the next afternoon together.

This caring seemed to spill over into the off-season. Not with Glenn, mind you, but with the rest of the team, which slowly began to jell.

* * *

At draft time there was a sense of uneasiness between the fan base and the media. Draft day wasn't a great day during the Bobby Grier/Pete Carroll era. Fans remember the Patriots got virtually nothing for the bevy of draft picks the team received for allowing Parcells to escape to the New York Jets following the 1996 Super Bowl.

Even Belichick's first draft wasn't eye-opening.

The team had to send its first-round pick to the Jets in a deal that allowed Belichick to be free of his Jets contract. Belichick's first pick was Klemm in the second round; the guy never got healthy or with the program.

The Patriots had the sixth pick in the draft. That was the highest since taking Glenn with the seventh selection overall in 1996.

The majority sentiment in the media was for taking Michigan's David Terrell. The Patriots needed weapons for Bledsoe. There was uncertainty about Glenn, as fans and media anticipated more problems with the wide receiver after he hadn't taken part in the off-season conditioning program. But the Patriots, never tipping their hand, had other things in mind. They needed a replacement for Eaton and a young interior lineman they could build with.

After the Browns took the best defensive lineman, Gerard Warren, off the board, Richard Seymour, 6'6", 305 pounds, out of Georgia, was the choice. He was a talented player, but two red flags immediately went up. One, he was not a nose tackle but more a tackle who played off the guard. And two, he had never played Belichick's two-gap style.

But the Patriots had done their homework. The team had hired Lionel Vital to be top scout and eventually elevated him to assistant college scouting director. Vital had come from the Jets, where he worked for Pioli and Parcells. Vital's presence suddenly turned the fortunes of the Patriots draft picks. He could really spot talent. As Seymour began to learn the system and get more comfortable with it, it was clear that Belichick and Pioli had finally hit one out of the park.

The Patriots were aggressive about maneuvering to get Matt Light, a big tackle that had protected Drew Brees at Purdue. Pioli moved up, down, and sideways. At the last moment, just as the enemy Jets were about to take Light, Pioli made a deal that gave the Patriots the 50th pick in the second round, one spot ahead of New York.

Light, like Seymour, gradually learned the system. He battled a training-camp ankle injury, but before long he had leaped over Klemm and veteran Grant Williams, and he was the team's starting left tackle, replacing Armstrong.

The only other player drafted that year who contributed somewhat was Leonard Myers, a talented cornerback. The rest of the picks will likely be heard from this season. Notre Dame corner Brock Williams (third round), Notre Dame tight end Jabari Holloway (fourth round), South Carolina State tight end Arther Love (fifth round), Washington safety Hakim Akbar (sixth round and later cut), were pretty much red-shirted because of injuries and inexperience.

But the bottom line was that the Patriots got two starters out of their draft. From there they mixed in veterans.

As training camp was about to start at Bryant College in Smithfield, Rhode Island, there weren't many thinking this would be the Cinderella team it became. A rough start to training camp didn't change that feeling, but behind the scenes, it was a team developing a quiet confidence.

CHAPTER 3

Camp Tragedy

"WANTED: WINNERS." That was the popular T-shirt worn by players during their restful moments as they walked about campus in the heat and humidity of Bryant College in Smithfield, Rhode Island. Belichick was big on subtle and not-so-subtle inducements to get his players to play at least to their level and hopefully beyond.

Belichick proved a master at revealing just the right motivational tool at the right time. While some teams go bowling during camp to bond as a team, Belichick had other ideas.

The coach and his wife, Debby, had watched the IMAX film *Shackleton's Voyage of Endurance*, set in the year 1915. It's the story of a crew's survival against every obstacle imaginable after their ship, *Endurance*, is trapped in ice and later crushed.

"I thought it was timely. I thought the team would learn something from watching it," said Belichick. "The bottom line was how those guys held together and supported each other. Guys had to give up things they wanted for the good of the group."

He loaded up the buses and made the trip to Providence, where the team watched the film. As usual with these field trips, some players watched with interest, while others fell asleep. Apparently, enough of them got the message, and the ones who fell asleep were probably the ones who were cut.

While that theme gradually built and seeped into the consciousness of players, it was starting out as the "Camp from Hell." Everything that could go wrong went wrong. If ever you could say with reasonable authority "This team is going nowhere," it was at the start of Patriots training camp.

Top receiver Terry Glenn was suspended by the league for a substance abuse policy violation. Veteran guard Joe Panos, penciled in as the starting right guard, retired suddenly. Andy Katzenmoyer, the team's former No. 1 draft choice in 1999, went AWOL, concerned over the pain in his surgically repaired neck. And the offensive line was already going down: Mike Compton had injured his calf and would be out for an extended period; Matt Light hurt his ankle; Damien Woody banged up his knee; and Adrian Klemm, who was favored at this point to win the left tackle spot, hurt his elbow.

However, these problems all paled in comparison to the real-life tragedy that swept through this country campus on August 6. Quarterback coach Dick Rehbein, 45, died of heart failure at Massachusetts General Hospital.

Rehbein suffered from cardiomyopathy, a disease of the heart muscle, and had worn a pacemaker. He had coached in the league for 23 years with the Green Bay Packers, the Los Angeles Express, the Minnesota Vikings, and the New York Giants. He left behind his wife, Pam, and his daughters, Betsy and Sarabeth.

"The greatest loss is to his wife and his two daughters," said Bledsoe. "He was first and foremost a family man. Every time we came into his office, he wanted to know about our family."

One of his best friends in life and in the coaching ranks was Weis, the Patriots offensive coordinator. He and Bledsoe quickly sprang into action and set up a trust fund to take care of the family after

Rehbein died. Bledsoe suggested the team earmark funds from player fines during the season for the fund. By season's end, the fund was up around $140,000.

Whether it was in honor of Rehbein or simply because it was too late to bring in a new coach, Weis assumed some of those duties, while Belichick also became more involved in the day-to-day coaching of the quarterbacks. There was concern because Rehbein had done such a good job bringing along the team's two young quarterbacks, Michael Bishop and Tom Brady.

At that time, however, there was no plan for Brady to supplant Bledsoe. Huard was the backup quarterback. Belichick said time and time again in camp that there was no substitute for the game experience that Huard had and, "It's very hard to win in the NFL." Huard was 6–1 with the Dolphins as a starter.

That Weis and Belichick were able to bring Brady along as they did following the death of the team's quarterback coach is another substory of this incredible season. Belichick was able to get Brady thinking about what the defense was going to do to stop or foil him. That thought process went far in helping Brady understand opposing defenses and learn when to check off or audible based on what the defense was giving him.

Belichick stated that he could deal with Glenn being suspended and Katzenmoyer going through his neck problems, but Rehbein's death was different.

"Those are problems you just deal with as a coach, but losing Dick Rehbein was beyond that. That was tragic. That's something that took us off guard. Here's a man, a person, who was so much a part of our team and our family. It hurt all of us, and our main concern at that time was for Dick's family," said Belichick.

The entire team showed up for a beautiful service for Rehbein in Smithfield, Rhode Island. Many members of the New York Giants, another team Rehbein had coached and that had been in Foxboro for a joint practice with the Patriots, attended as well.

* * *

One of the feel-good stories in camp was the comeback attempt of Robert Edwards, who had suffered a major knee injury during a four-on-four flag football game on Waikiki Beach, Hawaii, on February 5, 1999, during Pro Bowl week.

Edwards had labored for two seasons on his own impossible journey back from a severe injury to his knee that left few doctors believing he would ever return to NFL football. Edwards had to learn to walk again. Then run. Then run fast. Then cut. Dedicated workouts at the University of Georgia and then under running coach Tom Shaw in New Orleans had brought him to the point where that was almost possible.

At the June minicamp, Belichick commented, "They're trying to keep up with Robert at this point." Belichick loved Edwards. He loved his dedication and commitment. He loved his work ethic. Nobody was rooting harder for an Edwards comeback than Belichick, because Edwards was a true-life example of the dedication and work ethic Belichick was trying to build in the early stages of training camp.

Edwards, who signed a five-year deal in 1998 with a $3.1 million signing bonus, failed the running test on July 23. This was somewhat of a blow, because it appeared that conditioning was far from Edwards' problem.

When Edwards was able to retake the test the next day with temperatures in the mid-90s and the humidity close to 70 percent, he passed. Edwards ran 20 60-yard sprints (with 30-second breaks in between) within the required eight-second limit.

As if Edwards hadn't been through enough, he developed a groin injury after the first day of camp. It kept him out for weeks. He had fallen way behind, and the question became how much longer could the Patriots wait? Realistically, he wasn't going to start. Not with the team signing Antowain Smith in late July and with the presence of J. R. Redmond, Kevin Faulk, and even Edwards' Georgia roommate, Patrick Pass.

Edwards attended tryouts with other teams, but he sat out his third consecutive year. He signed a one-year contract with the Miami Dolphins on March 6, 2002.

Andy Katzenmoyer was part of the old regime. Former Patriots GM Bobby Grier had taken him with the second pick in the first round—28th overall—in the 1998 draft. He'd come out of Ohio State with a reputation for being a tough guy, but his first couple of years with the Patriots, something just wasn't right.

Katzenmoyer suffered a neck injury the first week of the 1999 season, just after he'd replaced Ted Johnson as the starting middle linebacker after Johnson tore his left biceps in training camp. He played well enough for a rookie, but he wasn't the reckless player he'd been at Ohio State. That hurt his game.

When he arrived to camp in late July 2000, he took part in the team's first workout. He did not return the next day. He was AWOL.

"My sense is that he left. I don't think he was kidnapped, but I don't know," said Belichick.

Katzenmoyer wasn't answering his phone at his townhouse in southeastern Massachusetts. His BMW was parked outside, but he wasn't answering his door either.

Katzenmoyer returned to the team two days later. He confirmed that he had panicked when pain returned to the left side of his neck after a series of hits in practice. He apologized to Belichick and then had the Patriots' medical staff administer treatment to his neck. Katzenmoyer met with Patriots team physician Dr. Bertram Zarins and then met with neurosurgeons at Massachusetts General Hospital for more testing. He scheduled second and third opinions, and he eventually went to Dallas, where he had surgery to remove a bulging disk.

Katzenmoyer said the pain at practice was similar to the pain he felt prior to having the first surgery.

"Nothing that severe, but it was the beginning of it," said Katzenmoyer. "It began right at the beginning [of practice]. I just panicked, to be honest with you. Coming into camp, I thought everything was fine. I was looking forward to the first day, and then after this happened, I just panicked, and I just freaked out."

Katzenmoyer, who will attempt to resume his career in 2002, said he didn't think it was just one particular hit but a series of collisions that left him in pain. The inside linebacker position is perhaps the most violent one on the field. The collisions are enormous, both from the punishment Katzenmoyer administers and from the punishment dished out by 300-plus offensive linemen looking to take him out of the play.

"It's the same location as last year," said Katzenmoyer, who sports a nasty scar right down the middle of the posterior of his neck. "It's in the neck, left side. I'm not a doctor, so I don't know exactly where it's coming from, but it started in the neck and came down the left trap [trapezius], and that's when I noticed a problem."

In October 2001 he had another surgery, this time to fuse two vertebrae. When asked if he contemplated retiring, he said no.

*   *   *

Belichick was tough on the team for the first couple of weeks, trying to get them in shape and used to the hot conditions. But Korey Stringer's death changed that. The massive Vikings offensive lineman died of heat stroke at the Vikings' training camp in August. The league came under more scrutiny about hydration and the rigors of training camp. Because of that some of the two-a-days were scaled back. Belichick even gave the team a day or two off. If they were in pads for one session, they'd be in shorts in the afternoon. A lot of work was done and the Patriots were improving. Players were saying the right things, and everyone noticed a definite change in atmosphere among the team. Despite all that had happened, there was a sense of togetherness and concern for one another, far different from last season's psyche.

"When you're on a team like I am, you just know when things are going to be right," said Troy Brown. "I wasn't predicting a championship back then, but I knew we were going to be a good team. I think everyone knew it. I know people didn't believe us, but when we looked around the locker room, we were pretty happy with what we had."

CHAPTER 4

At Last, the Games

Gone were those long, hot, and humid two-a-days when it seemed like a mile walk in the hot sun to get to the practice fields at Smithfield. Day after day, watching the same thing. Fans in the crowd would ooh and aah when a quarterback and a receiver would hook up on a long throw, or when a defensive back would make an interception. Writers and columnists would find one good play and write it up as if it were the definitive moment of camp.

The games were finally beginning.

The Patriots had scrimmaged the New York Giants in joint practices on August 7 and 8. It didn't take an expert in "Pigskinology" to tell which team had played in the Super Bowl the previous year. The Patriots didn't have Michael Strahan anywhere that I could see. The Giants looked faster and tougher.

But like everything else in this improbable season, the Patriots didn't need Michael Strahan. And beauty was certainly in the eye of the beholder.

In a night game at Foxboro Stadium on the warm, sticky, and rainy evening of August 10 before 45,125, the Patriots shut out the Giants, 14–0. Of course, everyone played it down. The Giants were just warming up, while the Patriots won with a bunch of scrubs. The Patriots were given credit for holding the Giants to 92 total yards.

Belichick played a lot of people, including the star of the game, kicker Owen Pochman, who didn't even make the team. Pochman, a seventh-round pick out of Brigham Young, kicked four field goals of 53, 23, 25, and 20 yards. Pochman kicked so well, the Giants eventually signed him after the Patriots cut him later in camp. Super Bowl hero Adam Vinatieri took the night off.

Belichick wanted to create competition at every position. Though he had one of the top kickers in the league in Vinatieri, he wanted to send Vinatieri the message that even he had room to improve.

Vinatieri's kickoffs weren't the greatest, even though he had spent the off-season with kicking guru Doug Blevins to improve his distance. For a while there was even speculation Belichick might keep Pochman for kickoffs. When Vinatieri showed he was kicking better, Pochman was let loose.

"Just to see how far he's come and to know that we work on mechanical things in the off-season that he's now applying in the games is something to watch," said Blevins. "Adam is a heck of a kicker. To make that [Super Bowl–winning kick] and the others he made in the playoffs showed his place among kickers in the league. He's right at the top."

Blevins coaches Miami's Olindo Mare full-time, but he believes the sky is the limit for Vinatieri. He even believes Vinatieri could become a Hall of Famer when all is said and done, because of his ability to make the big kick in crunch time.

"He really works at it," said Blevins. "He's from South Dakota State so people think you can kick in snow. But you have to work on making kicks in snow to do it. Adam leaves no stone unturned. Every off-season we work on something new. It was especially challenging last off-season because of the new balls that kickers use. We had to get used to that and Adam didn't miss a beat."

Blevins worked on Vinatieri's kickoffs, especially the hang time, and Vinatieri was much better at it toward the end of the season.

"I noticed it," said Blevins. "It's neat to see the work you do together pay off."

Blevins said there are a lot of comparisons between Vinatieri and Mare in that "they both have great legs and powerful and fast legs. They're two of the best in the game."

The Patriots offensive line for the scrimmage was makeshift to say the least. Due to a variety of injuries, future starters Compton (calf), Joe Andruzzi (back), and Klemm (shoulder) were all missing from the lineup in that first preseason game. Light was out with an ankle injury. On defense, Brandon Mitchell (quad) and Willie McGinest (back) didn't play. The Patriots started Adam Davis at one guard and veteran Grant Williams at left tackle.

Damien Woody, who has this problem about long snapping, snapped one at Bledsoe's knees, sending the quarterback scrambling back to retrieve the loose ball. Belichick wasn't happy that Woody couldn't perform a "junior high" exercise, though Woody's excellent talent as a run blocker and a pass protector more than compensated. Woody, who had a terrific season, had to relinquish his center duties during the shotgun during the regular season and move to left guard, switching with Compton.

Despite the problems, Bledsoe went three for four for 37 yards and was sacked twice by Strahan and Ryan Hale in six passing attempts before Belichick came to the conclusion that getting his starting quarterback killed probably wasn't the smartest thing he could do in early August. If Bledsoe had stayed in and Strahan kept playing, the All-Pro defensive end, who wound up setting the sack record, probably would have had about 20 sacks in this game alone and set the single-game record! Instead, Belichick brought in Huard, who went 9 for 12 for 85 yards. Thank goodness Strahan also called it a night.

Brady's first playing time of the 2001 preseason started in the third quarter when he drove the team 76 yards on 12 plays and set the stage for a Pochman field goal.

By now, the Giants weren't exactly playing their first string, but good things were coming from Brady and from running back

Antowain Smith, who broke loose for a 27-yard run in the third quarter.

Without Glenn, who was still AWOL, Patriots quarterbacks threw to 14 receivers and completed 60 percent of their passes, though none of them went for more than 22 yards.

The Philadelphia rejects were banged up in the game. Small suffered a gash in his leg and needed stitches, and Johnson got poked in the eye. Journeyman Curtis Jackson caught three passes for 40 yards and called the Patriots receiving core deep.

But it was David Patten, a former Giant, who began to distinguish himself in the receiver core when he completely turned around a Giant defender and streaked down the right sideline toward the end zone where Bledsoe overthrew him.

"David played well," lauded Belichick. "We had a shot for him on the first series. He had two yards of separation. It was a walk-in touchdown. He did that a number of times against the Giants. Anytime you have a vertical threat like that on the field, that's good."

Later, Patten, who started behind Brown, Johnson, and Emanuel on the depth chart, made a diving catch toward the sideline on a comeback pattern from Huard.

Defensively, the Patriots held the Giants to seven first downs.

They pressured Kerry Collins to death. Linebacker Matt Chatham even scored a safety when he tackled running back Omar Bacon in the end zone with 8:41 left.

Bryan Cox, wearing No. 0, signed just a few days prior to the game, intercepted a Collins pass and returned it 10 yards in the first quarter. The irony there is that in his debut interview he told the media he didn't think he could cover anyone anymore.

Richard Seymour, who had his head shaved in a rookie ritual earlier in the week, recorded two tackles and got some rushes on Giant quarterbacks. He got thumbs-up from Belichick.

Four field goals and a safety aren't the usual formula for winning football. But it was a good start.

"I knew after we played the Giants that we had more depth than they did," said Belichick. "We didn't have anyone like Strahan for sure, but we had overall better depth than a team that had gone to the Super Bowl."

An interesting week ensued. Glenn was placed on the reserve/left-camp list for the season and the popular Michael Bishop was released.

Bishop simply had fallen to fourth on the QB depth chart, and though the Patriots had kept four QBs in 2000, Bishop has become more of a distraction than anything. He was claimed by Green Bay, which had first dibs over Miami, which also made a claim. Green Bay kept him around for a couple of days and then released him. In the meantime, Miami traded with Chicago for Cade McNown, and Bishop never hooked on until he signed with the Canadian Football League's Toronto Argonauts in March 2002.

The Patriots made a play for Bears nose tackle Mike Wells, who had been released, but missed out.

They were off to Charlotte for Game 2 of the preseason against the Carolina Panthers. The Patriots seemed to pick up where they left off against the Giants. They beat the Panthers, 23–8, before 51,102 at Ericsson Stadium, raising their preseason record to 2–0. The Patriots scored their first two offensive touchdowns, and neither involved Bledsoe, perhaps an omen.

This was the real eye-opening game for Brady. The former Michigan standout completed 11 for 18 for 122 yards and one touchdown, a 16-yard pass to David Patten after relieving Bledsoe following the first series of the game.

Baltimore Ravens scout Terry McDonough was at the game that evening. As he and I sat at halftime over a hot dog and Coke he made the comment, "Brady is really poised. He looks like he can really play."

McDonough is one of the best talent evaluators in the business. His scouting produced Ray Lewis, Jamal Lewis, Priest Holmes, Jermaine Lewis, Duane Starks, and several others of the current

Ravens, which had won Super Bowl XXXV over the Giants. Maybe the Patriots knew what McDonough had just realized, but coming from an unbiased scout from another prominent organization, it seemed to carry weight with me.

It was the first game in which the Patriots showed a bit of balance in the offense: the running game produced 167 yards and the passing game 215. Patten, who had essentially replaced Glenn in the starting lineup, caught six passes for 65 yards. Smith began to separate himself from J. R. Redmond with 11 carries for 54 yards and a 22-yard run.

Patten's touchdown pass from Brady, which gave the Pats a 10–0 lead at the time, seemed a precursor as well. Brady began to see that what had been practiced was now working in games.

"It's a play we'd practiced all week that we've practiced all of camp. Our tight end on the play [Johnny McWilliams] cleared out the safety from the middle of the field, and David ran a terrific route and got himself open," said Brady.

There was also the first glimpse of trickery, which worked so well for the Patriots all season. The Pats used Cox as a blocking fullback on Redmond's one-yard touchdown run after practicing the formation all week in training camp.

But it was the defense that set the tone for this one when Law intercepted a Chris Weinke pass early in the game, setting up a 33-yard field goal by Vinatieri. Law, at that point of preseason, was called "one of the most improved players in camp" by Belichick. Law was definitely grasping the ins and outs of how to play in Belichick's defensive backfield. Though it wasn't all man-to-man, as Law preferred, he was excelling in the Cover-2 scheme, which would bode well later.

In addition, Seymour continued to show something more. With his 6'6" wingspan, he batted down two passes. But he also caught Belichick's wrath when he failed to come out for the extra-point team in the third quarter when the Panthers were going for two points. Seymour's brain cramp left the Patriots with only 10 men on the field.

"We had to blow a timeout," said Belichick. "We need to get him out on the field when the defense is out there."

After the game, the coach rewarded the team by announcing he was breaking camp, leaving their summer home in Smithfield for the uncomfortable confines of Foxboro Stadium.

Amid the upswing came a reminder of how cold the sport can be. Before the team boarded the bus to travel to the airport for their August 25 game against Tampa, Robert Edwards was informed he had been released.

"We just ran out of time," said Belichick. "You try to do what's best for your football team. You try to put the team first. It's not about what anyone wants to do. Robert Edwards is a tremendous athlete and competitor, and we wish him well."

That night, in a 20–3 loss to the Bucs in the all-important third game of the preseason schedule, Patriots backs carried 18 times for 39 yards. Their lead runner was fullback Marc Edwards with 22 yards.

Granted, the Bucs were considered to have one of the best defenses in the NFL coming into last season. But they made the patchwork Patriots offensive line look silly. Suddenly, whatever optimism had been built up was lost.

"I think we have a better team than what we showed," said Belichick. "There were too many lapses in all areas. We gave up too much on the opening kickoff and too many big plays against the defense. Offensively, we had trouble all day. We didn't play well. It's disappointing."

Poor Bledsoe could have used a suit of armor for this one to fend off Warren Sapp and Simeon Rice. At one point he was seen talking to Sapp and telling him, "Keep out of my backfield!" In five quarters of playtime to this point in the preseason, he had been sacked six times. Not a healthy ratio.

The Patriots certainly had a good measure of how far they needed to go in a short time. They still had Compton and Light out of the lineup, and Klemm was still hurt.

"Getting five guys working together as a unit was a priority coming into the season, so I think that's a concern," said Woody. "Last season we were a shambles for most of the season. But we have a week and a half before the regular season. Hopefully, some of our injured guys can get healthy."

Bledsoe didn't come out of the game until 50 seconds remained in the third quarter. He went 10 for 21 for 82 yards. The offense managed four first downs in the first three quarters and went 1 for 10 on third-down conversions. The Patriots defense couldn't stop the slippery Warrick Dunn, who gained 115 yards on 12 carries including long runs of 35 and 56 yards.

The best that could be said about this one is that Bledsoe escaped without injury.

It was the officials who were on strike, but a wise guy would say the Patriots offensive line was as well against Tampa. But there was one more chance to get it together before the regular season.

On August 30, playing the final preseason game ever at Foxboro Stadium, which was torn down at the end of the season and turned into a parking lot for the new CMGI Field, the Patriots let it all hang out in a 33–13 win before 48,911.

The Redskins were without Bruce Smith and Champ Bailey, but Bledsoe was sharp, completing 14 of 22 for 145 yards and one touchdown, and helped the offense amass 382 yards. Roman Phifer led the defense, without question one of the most significant free-agent signings. Phifer had two sacks, two forced fumbles, and one recovery. Vinatieri warmed up with field goals of 50, 52, 46, and 30 yards.

The Patriots also played without Law (foot) and Johnson (hip) and rested a banged up Bruschi. Light emerged as the front-runner for the starting left tackle job after a strong performance. Only Compton was missing now in what would become the starting offensive line.

Brady relieved Bledsoe and went 11 for 19 for 166 yards. He executed a perfect screen pass to Kevin Faulk that Faulk took to the house for 54 yards, the longest play from scrimmage in the preseason. It produced a few blank stares because it had been a while since anyone in New England had seen a perfectly executed screen pass.

On this day, *Forbes Magazine* released its annual study on all 31 NFL franchises and calculated the Patriots were worth $524 million, ninth overall, estimating revenue at $128 million. After they beat the Redskins their stock was surely rising.

Fans left Foxboro that night feeling that maybe this was a better team than had been advertised.

"The slate's clean now," said Belichick. "I don't think you have a comfort level at this time of the year. Everyone has to go out and establish things against game plans with our best people versus their best people."

* * *

OK, with a 3–1 preseason there was some optimism. Those of us who have been through football camps and baseball spring trainings know not to get too excited this time of the year.

Globe columnist Michael Holley was really the first to express his giddiness. At first I had to read through the article and make sure he wasn't kidding. He was serious. Good for him. He knew something the rest of us didn't.

In an August 31 column he wrote:

> *The real games begin in nine days, but all you hear now is how terrible the Patriots are going to be. The talk is of weak lines, questionable running backs, and flawed tight ends.*
>
> *There is a center that has long-snapping phobia. There is a suspended wide receiver that has a long-distance-calling phobia. And there is a receiver's agent, a wannabe Jerry Maguire, who has invisible*

exclamation points after most of his statements. He is going to sue the NFL (!). Paul Tagliabue didn't have the decency to warn him of his client's suspension (!). The head coach of the Patriots is out of control (!).

So you ask, what's next?

Answer: a season that should be better than what the majority expects.

Holley even suggested the Patriots would make the playoffs. What was he thinking?

Holley had a feeling. He was way out in front.

CHAPTER 5

The Impossible Game

There's a silly game sportswriters play when the season starts. We look down the schedule and find the wins and the losses.

Game 1 versus Cincinnati? Pretty split through Patriots Nation.

Some thought the Bengals, the Patriots' first opponent, were much improved. They were playing at home and, of course, the Bengals should win. I thought that as well, but a Patriots win wouldn't have surprised me. After all, they were 3–1 in the preseason.

Somewhere in the back of our collective mind we thought they were a little better than we first thought. We knew they would play hard, never quit. We knew they could beat the mediocre teams, and the Bengals were certainly that.

Second game versus Carolina: OK, that was a win. Third game versus the Jets: loss. Fourth game versus the Colts: they have the Colts' number so let's say a win. At Miami: loss. Home versus San Diego: win. At Indianapolis: let's call it a loss and a split in the series. At Denver: loss. At Atlanta: win. Home against Buffalo: win. Home against St. Louis: loss. Home against New Orleans: loss. At the Jets: loss. Home against Cleveland: win. At Buffalo: loss. Home against Miami: last game, probably wouldn't mean much, but let's give the Patriots a split.

What does that come out to?

"We're going to prove you guys wrong," thumped Lawyer Milloy. "You watch what happens. We've got veterans and good players on this team. We're going to play hard every game and execute every game. You watch."

Certainly the division was vulnerable.

The Jets had hired the softer, gentler Herman Edwards, who had been Tony Dungy's right-hand man in Tampa Bay. The Jets had gone through the rough and tough approach of Parcells and Al Groh, and quite frankly it hadn't worked as well as New Yorkers had hoped. Edwards was a breath of fresh air. All of the secrecy and tight lips were gone. Media was allowed to watch practice during the week. Heck, the team even invited the media to a barbecue with the players every Friday.

The Jets still had good players, including Curtis Martin, Vinny Testaverde, and Wayne Chrebet; a good, young offensive line; and a tough defense led by Mo Lewis, Marvin Jones, Aaron Glenn, and company. They were my choice to win the division.

The Colts, meanwhile, seemed the popular preseason choice. General manager Bill Polian had addressed the shaky defense somewhat in the off-season, though, as it turned out, not nearly enough. The Colts still had the most explosive offense with a Big Three of Peyton Manning, Edgerrin James, and Marvin Harrison and a top offensive line to protect Manning. But after a great start, the Patriots sent the Colts on a long downward spiral they would never recover from.

The Bills had a new coach—Gregg Williams—who had been the defensive coordinator at Tennessee under Jeff Fischer. They also had a new boss in Tom Donahoe of Pittsburgh Steelers fame, which right off the bat had to clear an enormous amount of cap space, letting several high-profile veterans go, including Doug Flutie, who lost his ongoing struggle with Rob Johnson.

So decimated, it didn't appear the Bills would be a factor.

The Fish always made the playoffs and they always fell a little short. They had a killer defense and weapons on offense, including the mobile Jay Fiedler at quarterback. But they were September Dolphins and January Shrimp.

There was an opening for the Patriots, but were they good enough to seize it?

Eddie Andelman, a pioneer sports-talk-show host in Boston for 30 years, had sensed something special for the Pats from the start. Eddie usually has good intuition on such things. For instance, in 1996 he had a personal campaign called "Jambalaya," referring to the popular New Orleans cuisine, in which the Patriots played and lost to the Green Bay Packers in Super Bowl XXXI. Prior to the 1996 season, Andelman had gone to Las Vegas to wager on the Patriots. He bet that the Patriots would win the division and the AFC championship and that they'd reach the Super Bowl and play Green Bay. Andelman won every tiebreaker and won the pool!

Andelman was a big supporter of the Boston sports teams, and he had a big stake in Patriots history in particular. He owned the parking lots on the Foxboro Stadium and Raceway property. He and his partners, Jim McCarthy and Mark Witkin, who at one time had the most popular talk show in Boston, *The Sports Huddle*, sold them to Kraft on May 17, 1996, for several million. But Andelman wasn't afraid to speak his mind if one of the players wasn't doing the right thing. Andelman certainly liked Drew Bledsoe personally, but he would often be heard saying, "He doesn't have *it*!"

It? What was *it?*

As soon as he saw Tom Brady he said, "This kid has *it*!"

After Bledsoe was injured in the second game of the season and Brady took over starting the third game, Andelman was heard saying over the airwaves, "Jambalaya!"

He was right again.

*   *   *

On September 3, 2001, the Patriots cut down to their final roster of 53. Well, almost. Gone were wide receivers Curtis Jackson, Sean

Morey, and Tony Simmons. Gone were tight ends Johnny McWilliams, who was the son-in-law of former USC and Rams coach John Robinson, and Harvard's Chris Eitzmann.

Sent packing were offensive lineman Drew Inzer of Brown University, who resurfaced on the practice squad offensive lineman Sale Isaia; and Josh Rawlings. Owen Pochman was cut. And the team placed running back Walter Williams, who had been impressive at minicamps and in training camp, on injured reserve.

Also seeing their final days with the Patriots were defensive lineman Garrett Johnson, linebacker Rob Holmberg, defensive back Kato Serwanga, and punter Brad Costello. Defensive lineman Dave Nugent was also cut but re-signed later. Veteran linebacker Marty "Mr. Irrelevant" Moore was cut but re-signed the next day when the Patriots decided to let pass rusher Greg Spires go. Spires later signed with Cleveland.

"This is probably the toughest day of the year for me," said Belichick. "There are a large number of guys we've spent significant amounts of time with either this year, last year, or previous years. These are guys that have worked hard, have given us everything they could. They weren't just taking up space; they were very competitive."

You had to feel bad for Sean Morey. He grew up in the South Shore beach town of Marshfield and attended Brown University. Morey is so smart he could have run the Patriots, let alone play for them.

His desire and work ethic matched his intelligence. He had been drafted in the seventh round in the 1999 draft and hung on the team's practice squad as a receiver. He had shown excellent ability as a gunner on special teams. He was always around the ball. As a wide receiver, he had a big-play quality about him. Not the biggest or fastest guy, but a winner. He had gone to NFL Europe and played for the Barcelona Dragons, where he started as a defensive back for former Boston College coach and Dragons coach Jack Bicknell. When he returned to Patriots camp, he was playing three ways: receiver, safety, and special teams.

It was hard to believe there wasn't a spot for Morey, a fan favorite. But in Belichick's top-10 list of things that are important when choosing a player, fan favorite didn't make the list. He considers the best players, regardless of their popularity.

Later, when Belichick learned the Philadelphia Eagles for the playoff run had picked up Morey, nobody was happier than Belichick. "Great kid. I'm real happy for him."

The final roster was comprised of three quarterbacks, five running backs, five receivers, two tight ends, nine offensive linemen, seven defensive linemen, eight linebackers, eleven defensive backs, and three special teamers.

Here's the team that started the season:

Quarterbacks: Drew Bledsoe, Tom Brady, and Damon Huard.

Running backs: Antowain Smith, Marc Edwards, Kevin Faulk, J. R. Redmond, and Patrick Pass.

Wide receivers: David Patten, Troy Brown, Charles Johnson, Torrance Small, and Bert Emanuel.

Tight end/half-backs: Rod Rutledge and Jermaine Wiggins.

Offensive line: Matt Light, Mike Compton, Adrian Klemm, Damien Woody, Joe Andruzzi, Greg Robinson-Randall, Kenyatta Jones, Grant Williams, and Grey Ruegamer.

Defensive line: Bobby Hamilton, Richard Seymour, Brandon Mitchell, Willie McGinest, Anthony Pleasant, Jace Sayler, and Riddick Parker.

Linebackers: Tedy Bruschi, Ted Johnson, Mike Vrabel, T. J. Turner, Larry Izzo, Roman Phifer, Marty Moore, and Bryan Cox.

Defensive backs: Ty Law, Terrell Buckley, Lawyer Milloy, Tebucky Jones, Otis Smith, Leonard Myers, Matt Stevens, Hakim Akbar, Terrance Shaw, Je'Rod Cherry, and Antwan Harris.

Special teams: Lee Johnson, Adam Vinatieri, and Lonie Paxton.

Belichick had changed close to half of the roster from the previous season—24 new faces. The coach kept 6 of his 10 draft choices, placing rookie tight ends Jabari Holloway and Arther Love on IR.

Oh, there'd be more tinkering along the way, but this was the team that started the season. It wasn't a roster rich with All-Pros, big names, and high-salaried players. It was a team of football players. Those who, in Belichick and Pioli's estimation, "loved playing football."

There were still questions.

Compton, who had a shaved head and a tattoo, still hadn't played a down. He had spent many years blocking for Barry Sanders in Detroit, and, watching him on film, Belichick and Pioli thought he'd add a real toughness to the line, almost a street fighter mentality. But at this point in the season, who knew what Compton would bring?

Light looked swell in the final preseason game, but was he ready for prime time?

"I thought Matt had a pretty decent game against Washington," said Belichick. "It was not great; there were some things he could have done better. But I thought overall he was aggressive on the run blocking and he did a decent job at handling the game."

How good was Seymour?

With Glenn serving a four-game suspension at the start of the season, would Brown and Patten be enough? The Patriots were desperately searching for a tight end to replace Ben Coates, but in 2000 none was found. Wiggins had showed promise at the end of 2000 with 12 catches in four games. Rutledge was a decent blocker, but he had hands of stone. The Patriots were going with a running back—Antowain Smith—who had been buried by the Bills, and a fullback—Marc Edwards—who couldn't get on the field with the Browns.

On defense, Belichick was banking on 36-year-old Otis Smith to play the right corner opposite Law. Was Tebucky Jones ever going to make it as a top free safety? Could McGinest and Ted Johnson stay healthy? Could Bruschi play another 1,200 plays as he had in 2000? Did Phifer, Cox, and Pleasant have anything left?

One thing Belichick was certain about was his backup quarterback. On September 4, Belichick announced five-year veteran Huard would have to take a step back to No. 3. The backup quarterback was Brady.

"I'm not saying the situation will be that way every week throughout the year," said Belichick. "But based on the preseason, we just feel like Tom, right now, is a little bit ahead of Damon in terms of handling the team."

Brady went 31 for 54 in the preseason games for 384 yards and two touchdown passes.

"I don't think there was any question in anybody's mind that Tom had clearly taken over the leadership of that entire group of last year's rookies—offense, defense, everybody that was involved," said Belichick. "I think he was well respected. Tom has a lot of natural leadership. It was something that all those players saw and looked up to, and it was a natural thing for him and he was very comfortable doing it."

Belichick made it clear that the organization wasn't down on Huard. The coaching staff felt Brady was further ahead after being in the second season of the offense.

"I think I approached it like I've always approached it," said Brady. "Whether I'd be No. 2 or No. 3, I'd be ready to play."

Huard took the news diplomatically, but it had to hurt.

"I've had some success in this league and I've won before, and I plan on doing that again," said Huard. "You just keep fighting. It's a long season, so you always have to be prepared to go."

A day later, Belichick announced the team's cocaptains. Bledsoe and Brown, the offensive players with the longest tenure with the team with nine years each, were named the offensive cocaptains. On defense, Milloy and Cox were named. Izzo was named the special-teams captain.

This announcement meant one major change. The oft-injured McGinest had been supplanted as a defensive cocaptain. After just 37 days Cox had already made an impact on his teammates.

"It's good for me that, just being there for a short time, your teammates think that highly of you," said Cox. "But regardless of being a captain or whatnot, my job is to lead, whether that's by example or by words. For me, that's [captain has] been my title wherever I've been."

In Cox's own words "the end is coming" after a long career with the Dolphins, the Bears, and the Jets, "so everything is a little more precious. But the thing that I've found is I've been able to have fun over the last couple of years because I act silly, and even in an intense situation where everybody else is tense, I'm laughing or telling a stupid joke because I'm enjoying it more.

"I know that every minute, every play, every day I get to do this is precious, because it's not going to last long."

Cox also proved his ability as a negotiator. Eyeing his old No. 51 throughout camp, he finally consummated a deal with fellow line-backer Mike Vrabel for the coveted number. Vrabel took No. 50.

Milloy had long been the leader of the defense. His hard hits and leadership on the field were contagious. He was never one to be afraid to tell a teammate he wasn't living up to his role.

Bledsoe and Brown were two of the quieter leaders. The position Bledsoe plays and the toughness he showed in playing hurt, getting knocked down more than 80 times and sacked 50 times the year before, showed his commitment to the team. Brown simply showed his leadership on the field. When the team needed a big play, Brown took it upon himself to provide it.

Izzo became special-teams leader—with the extra emphasis Belichick had on special teams, he was going to be an important cog in what was to come.

There wasn't a lot of pizzazz, but there was substance—no leading men, but a team of character actors who made this a movie to remember.

CHAPTER 6

An Impossible September

The fact that the Patriots lost their first two games, one before and one after September 11, seemed a blip on the radar screen. The carnage of lost lives was gruesome at ground zero at the World Trade Center in New York and at the Pentagon in Washington, D.C.

Our country stopped in shock. Sports became completely irrelevant, except for its diversion. Players, coaches, and management echoed that sentiment.

Some sports types believed that life should go on and that our country should not allow the perpetrators of this heinous act to feel they had disrupted our society and culture. It was a sound theory, but the reality was that Americans didn't feel like doing anything except mourning the loss of the casualties and redirecting their energies toward the common goal of being a united country, a team, if you will.

That the Red Sox were unfolding before our eyes was no longer front-page news. That the NFL officials couldn't reach a contract agreement was so trivial. That the Patriots had lost their opener . . . who really cared?

Patriotism was strong, and it seemed to provide us with a real-life example of togetherness and teamwork. This was not lost on the New England Patriots, who felt the effects of the tragedy as closely as any team in the NFL.

Patriots' right guard Joe Andruzzi was living it all right.

Andruzzi's brothers, Billy, Marc, and Jimmy, are all New York City firefighters who were helping with the rescue mission. Joe Andruzzi, who hails from Staten Island, New York, frantically phoned everyone he knew associated with his brothers, but he couldn't get through.

Hours went by. Panic filled his heart. He knew they were around it, maybe in it.

Finally, he got a call from Engine 5, assuring him his brothers were OK. In fact, they had become real-life heroes, rescuing hundreds of people from the burning and collapsing refuse.

"It was very stressful," said Andruzzi, who was sobbing as he told the story. "It was stressful trying to call my family. I was calling and hearing a message: 'Due to a tornado warning . . .' I just kept getting busy signals. It was a few hours before I could reach my parents."

Jimmy, 30, worked at Engine 5 on East 14th Street at the fire station closest to the World Trade Center and was one of the first of 500 firefighters to respond after the first tower was struck. The company had just put out a blaze on East 19th Street.

When they got there, Tower 2 had just been hit.

Jimmy's duty was to go all the way up to the 79th floor of Tower 1, where the flames and damage were most intense, and do what he could to save lives. On his way up, his superiors radioed him to say that another firefighter was having chest pains and perhaps a heart attack on the 20th floor. It might be that rerouting that saved Jimmy Andruzzi's life.

He tended to his fellow firefighter and brought him down 20 flights through black smoke and out the door just as the building was crumbling.

"The hardest part was trying to find them," said Joe Andruzzi. "Because Jimmy was right next to the Trade Center, I thought he'd be one of the first ones called. I couldn't get ahold of anybody. They were saying not to call, but how could you not? Once I got ahold of him, there were guys passing cell phones, calling families just to say, 'I'm OK.'"

Andruzzi called his brother in the days after the tragedy and "he was pretty shook up." There were 200 firefighters missing at the time and many were friends of the Andruzzi family.

Andruzzi said his mother was "hysterical crying" even though she knew her sons had made it out OK. "I can't blame her," said Andruzzi.

Billy and Marc Andruzzi worked multiple shifts in attempts to rescue and recover bodies. All of the Andruzzis attended several funerals. Jimmy Andruzzi knew as many as 75 people who died.

Two players—Roman Phifer and Greg Robinson-Randall—didn't make it back the day after the tragedy because airports were closed. At the time, the NFL still hadn't canceled games for that Sunday. Phifer had returned home to Los Angeles to visit his son. Robinson-Randall had gone to Texas. Robinson-Randall wound up taking a 36-hour bus trip to get back to Foxboro.

The Patriots had suspended operations for a couple of days, and then on September 13 the NFL finally ruled the games were going to be canceled.

"I think everybody fully understands why we did what we did, and we're supportive of it," said Belichick. "I told the players and coaches that this would be a time for us to reflect and grieve, then try to put it behind us. I think it's important for players to spend time with their families and their loved ones, and I think they should do that. It's pretty obvious that traveling now is not going to be too predictable, so I encourage them to stay as close as they possibly could or make plans to be here by Sunday. And if they travel, travel by car."

The players were relieved not to have to play so soon after the tragedy. After all, there was a true feeling of uneasiness in the country. Major League Baseball had taken the lead in suspending games as soon as the tragedy occurred, and there was a national security concern for venues holding 50,000 to 70,000 people.

"America is distraught right now, not knowing what's going on," said Andruzzi. "People can't really focus. You're risking injury to players who are going to be out there not being focused on the game. I think it's the right decision. Guys just need time to take it all in, then start back up next week."

Ted Johnson disagreed with all of the life-goes-on sentiment and was pleased with the ruling.

"Something did happen, and it's huge," said Johnson, speaking at his locker in the old Patriots locker room. "It's a huge tragedy. For us to dismiss our feelings about it, I don't think that's right. Out of respect for the people involved and their families, I think our nation needs to grieve. I think our nation needs to feel the impact of what's happened here."

*   *   *

The regular season had opened on September 9 in Cincinnati with a 23–17 loss. It was hot and humid at Paul Brown Stadium, but that didn't excuse the fact that the Patriots didn't play 60 minutes of football. That pretty much summarized the problem in their early losses.

The Patriots' top two rookies didn't start. Seymour didn't play at all, left behind in Foxboro to nurse his hamstring injury. Sayler, a nose tackle from Michigan State, replaced him as the Patriots opened the year in a 3-4 alignment on defense. Light, who all assumed would start, backed up Williams and didn't see action until the fourth quarter. Light had brought a busload of friends from a Greenville, Ohio, church he belonged to who thought they'd be watching their guy. Belichick had other ideas.

Late Saturday night Belichick had a revelation on Light. It had been reported that Light was being punished for something, but Belichick said, "I didn't think he was ready to start."

Once Light got into the game he played OK, but then he sprained his right ankle when he was rolled over on a block.

The Patriots were also missing longtime radio commentator Gino Cappelletti, one of the greatest players in the team's history and a longtime broadcasting partner of Gil Santos, the voice of the Patriots. Cappelletti had had heart surgery at Massachusetts General Hospital and was replaced by former Patriots center Peter Brock.

Even worse, Johnson, the team's top run-stopper at the time, had suffered a hip flexor injury August 25 against the Tampa Bay Bucs while playing on a punt team, and even though he tried to play, coaches held him out after he experienced pain in pregame warm-ups.

Not a good sign.

The Patriots were a little ticked off right before the game began because Cincinnati public-address announcer Tom Kinder was announcing the names of the defense while everyone was still in the locker room. Kinder was trying to keep to a schedule, and the Patriots were a little late.

Milloy thought the Bengals were being disrespectful and said, "The hell with it. Let's just run out there as a team." And of course the ritual that the team came to be known by began by accident. In the weeks to come, the Patriots did it differently each week, sometimes coming out as an offensive unit or a defensive unit. Eventually they just came out as a team.

Not that it did much good against the Bengals.

It was indeed a frustrating day for Patriots Nation.

Bobby Hamilton's postgame scream, heard through the concrete walls of the Patriots locker room, might have been the quote that summed up the day for the Patriots.

There were many frustrating moments, none more head-scratching than the run defense's inability to stop Corey Dillon, who rattled off a 40-yard run en route to 104 yards on 24 carries. He had 86 yards on 13 carries in the first half alone. With Seymour and Johnson out, Dillon had a field day in the first half, but the Patriots, who actually led the game 10–3 in the second quarter, were saved by the fact that Bengals offensive coordinator Bob Bratkowski didn't give Dillon the ball more. He kept allowing Jon Kitna to pass. Thanks, Bob.

"He's a beast," said Law of Dillon.

He was a beast who would have gained 200 yards had he got the ball more, but Bratkowski's play calling allowed the Patriots to stay in the game.

Bryan Cox, who was filling in for Johnson, let tight end Tony McGee out of his sight and McGee made him pay—a 25-yard touchdown pass from Kitna in the third quarter, which made it a 23–10 game.

"I made too many plays I wished I could have had back," lamented Cox. "We showed resiliency in coming back, but I made a bonehead play letting the tight end free for a touchdown."

"We tackled like crap," said Law. "We prepared all week for Dillon. We knew what we were up against, and we let him off the hook."

The Patriots disappeared in the third quarter—nine plays, no first downs. But with 9:17 remaining in the game, Bledsoe got into a rhythm. He directed an 11-play, 94-yard drive using predominantly a no-huddle offense.

Three passes went to Brown for 9, 31, and 12 yards as Brown caught seven passes for 126 yards, beginning his tremendous season in which he caught 101 passes. Bledsoe found Wiggins for 12 more before finding Wiggins for eight yards to close the gap to 23–17. Wiggins broke tackles to get there and then lunged to the goal line. The replacement officials used instant replay to review the play and let the touchdown ruling stand.

"I was definitely in the end zone," said Wiggins, the pride of East Boston. "I just needed to make a play right there by breaking tackles. I had the ball all the way."

Momentum was all New England's at this point.

With a six-point lead, the Bengals were still trying to pass rather than run out the clock with Dillon. But that was fine with the Patriots.

After the Bengals went three-and-out, the Patriots had the ball with 3:57 remaining at their own 30-yard line.

The Patriots managed one first down and advanced to the Bengals' 41. But it was fourth-and-2. Obviously, the Patriots had to go for it. So Bledsoe, trying to catapult his 6'6" frame, lunged forward on a quarterback sneak. The spot was less than generous, and the Patriots had turned the ball back to the Bengals.

"It was my call," admitted Bledsoe, who completed 22 of 38 for 241 yards, two touchdowns, and no interceptions. "I thought I had put the ball out there enough to get the first down."

Belichick was questioned about why he didn't challenge the spot on the field. There was more than two minutes remaining so he had the right.

"There were so many bodies around, we didn't want to use a timeout to challenge, feeling we'd need the timeouts later," responded Belichick.

There was still time. The Bengals took over at their 40. In fact, Bratkowski finally did what he should have and called handoffs to Dillon for three runs. This time the Patriots defense was ready. He lost six yards, and the Bengals had to punt.

With 1:54 to go, Bledsoe had time to pull out a fourth-quarter come-back, of which he had 14 in his career. But Takeo Spikes, one of the best linebacker's in the game, sacked the quarterback for a seven-yard loss. On the next play Bledsoe looked to complete a 15-yard pass to Emanuel, but replay officials watched the video and ruled Emanuel had trapped the ball. On fourth-and-17, Bledsoe rolled to his left, but Adrian Ross slammed Bledsoe to the grass as he tried to get rid of the ball.

"We couldn't get the end sealed," said Belichick, "and that's the guy who eventually came in there. We were trying to hold the ball and throw it downfield. We needed 18 yards. We had to try to get the receivers more time to get down there. Eventually, they chased him down."

While the Patriots game was going, the Colts had dismantled the Jets, 45–24, using a hurry-up offense to score 28 points in the second quarter. While Doug Flutie was leading his new team, the Chargers, to a 30–3 win over Washington, the Bills and Rob Johnson were getting trounced by the Saints, 24–6.

*   *   *

After the September 11 tragedy, the NFL resumed on September 23. The canceled games were replayed January 1, 2002, and the NFL eventually worked it out with the city of New Orleans to move the Super Bowl back a week to February 3.

At the time the Patriots were thought to have caught a break not having to play the Carolina Panthers in Charlotte because the Panthers had upset the Minnesota Vikings 24–13 in week one. But the Patriots were playing the New York Jets at home in a star-spangled atmosphere where patriotism was never greater and where unity among the fans was at an all-time high.

The Patriots, already cited as the premier team in the league in the area of security, tightened it up even more. Fans, and in some cases, their cars, were searched thoroughly as they entered Foxboro Stadium for a 4:00 P.M. start. Nobody seemed to mind.

Fans were shouting "USA! USA!" at least an hour before the game even began. The Andruzzi family was honored at halftime, and Olympic hero of the 1980 "Miracle on Ice" team Jim Craig presented the family a replica of the flag that Craig had carried after the U.S. team's chilling win over Russia.

Craig has special meaning to me. I had covered him in the "Miracle on Ice" quest as a young reporter. It was fitting that Craig, part of one of the most chilling moments in American sports history, was involved in something so American and so patriotic.

Bill Andruzzi, Joe, Jimmy, Billy, and Marc's father, a New York City cop most of his life, had worked a detail in Lake Placid for that event and appreciated Craig's gesture. "It meant a lot to my boys to see Jim Craig down there today," said the elder Andruzzi.

It was an emotional day for everyone. In some ways the playing of this game meant life was resuming as normal as it could be. There were heavy hearts in the stands, in the press box, and on the field. Vinny Testaverde's father, a mason by trade, had helped build the twin towers 30 years before. Curtis Martin and some of his teammates had visited ground zero and came away different people.

How could there be as much emotion during the game as there was before it?

The crowd continued its chants of "USA! USA! USA!" as the flag was unfurled at midfield. The fans sang "America the Beautiful" and accompanied Massachusetts State Trooper Dan Clark in "The Star-Spangled Banner." The *Globe*'s Frank Dell'Appa caught up with season-ticket holders Brian and Jamie McDonough of Dedham, Massachusetts, in Section 316 where in the back row of the stadium they held a huge American flag with 48 stars. "The flag has been in our family for a long time," said Brian McDonough. "It was given to us when our uncle, Robert McDonough, died in World War II."

There was a sense of camaraderie. Normally Patriots and Jets fans mix like oil and water, but while they rooted for their team, they knew after the events of September 11 that they were really on the same team.

CHAPTER 7

0-and-Drew

To this day, former New York Jets cornerback Aaron Glenn, who was on the field the moment Jets linebacker Mo Lewis nearly ended Drew Bledsoe's career and life with a hard, clean, sideline hit, claims, "To be honest, I'd seen Mo deliver bigger hits than that before. We never thought that hit would lead to the problems Drew wound up having. We were all concerned about him afterward. You never want to hurt a player like that, even if he is a rival."

Brady, on the sideline that day, had a different view: "It was one of the hardest hits I'd ever seen. I could hear it. His entire face mask was turned around on his head and it was bent."

It was not dirty, or roughing the passer, or anything remotely borderline. Bledsoe was rolling to his right trying to make a play. When that wasn't possible he tried to get out of bounds, but he did so upright, making no attempt to slide to protect his body. This had been a common scene in Bledsoe's last two seasons in which he'd been sacked 100 times in 1999 and 2000 alone. If he was going to get hurt, everyone assumed it would have been then. Not now.

On September 23 the Patriots were losing 10–3 with 4:48 remaining when the blow occurred. Bledsoe took the hit flush to the left side of his body. After lying fairly still for a few moments, he picked himself up and went to the sideline.

Grant Williams, who replaced the injured Robinson-Randall at right tackle that day, had been running a few yards behind when he saw Bledsoe's face as he rose from the ground. What he saw was a man who looked very dazed. His instincts took over and he yelled "Brady!"

Bledsoe reentered the game for another series, but it became painfully obvious something was wrong. When Bledsoe started speaking to Huard on the sideline, it was gibberish.

"He was asking me about plays that he should have known like the back of his hand," recalled Huard.

At that point, Huard let the medical staff know that Bledsoe wasn't right. He was obviously suffering from a concussion, but the Patriots medical staff and coaches never used that word. They said he "got his bell rung."

"I shouldn't have put him out there," said Belichick. "He was out. Watching him play after the hit, I just didn't think he was himself."

After the game, more symptoms cropped up, trouble breathing being the main one. Something was going on inside Bledsoe's jolted body.

When he got to the hospital after the game had ended, it was determined—just in time—that Bledsoe was bleeding internally. His chest cavity was filling with blood. The source of it was the next problem to solve. Massachusetts General doctors quickly went to work and found that Bledsoe had a sheared blood vessel in his lung. Because Massachusetts General Hospital is such an advanced facility, it was able to recycle Bledsoe's lost blood back into his body. With a tube down his chest sucking out the blood to prevent further internal damage, Bledsoe lost seven pints in 24 hours, more than half the blood in his body.

The Bledsoe bashers, who had grown in numbers, were probably concerned about his health, but a segment of the Patriots fandom had grown tired of the man who saved the franchise in 1993. They didn't care for his lack of mobility or for his ability to occasionally throw an interception at the worst time. The bashers had hoped that prior to signing his 10-year, $103 million deal in March the Patriots would trade him and sign another quarterback.

The bashers weren't thinking straight. The offensive line that nearly got him killed against the Jets was even worse the two previous seasons. Four-fifths of the line that started in 2000 was out of football, a point that Borges brought out often. And it was true.

If Bledsoe was going to be out for a long time—and he was—then many fans were ready for the next chapter. They were certainly skeptical that Brady would be the man. In the previous season the mobile Michael Bishop had been the heartthrob of some fans and players on the team who believed Bishop should get more playing time. But Bishop was gone.

Brady's indoctrination into that September 23 game wasn't anything fancy. In fact, Belichick came up to Brady and said, "Drew's out and you're in."

When Brady came into the game, nobody knew that Bledsoe had been injured. That's because CBS sideline reporter Bonnie Bernstein had been told by the Patriots public relations staff, which had been told by the medical staff, that replacing Bledsoe was a "coach's decision." CBS analyst Dan Dierdof ran with it. The entire nation now thought that Bledsoe had been replaced due to a benching, when in fact he was hurt badly.

All of it was sorted out after the game, but at this moment young Brady had 2:16 to carve out a miracle finish, starting at the Patriots' 26.

Brady threw for a couple of first downs, a 21-yard pass to David Patten being the most significant. But a pair of passes toward the end zone on the game's final two plays didn't connect, and the Patriots had bowed to the Jets, 10–3, to start their 2001 campaign 0–2.

"I knew we needed a touchdown to tie the game," said Brady. "The last play was pretty close. Everyone was out fighting to the last play. Hopefully we won't be in position too often where it goes down to the last play."

Brady did one thing a little better than Bledsoe: he had slid out of bounds with Lewis coming at him.

"You are just trying to get out of bounds and get as much yardage as you can in that situation," said Brady. "I've played a lot of football, and if I got hit that hard I would be in the hospital for a month. That shows you how big and tough and strong that guy [Bledsoe] is."

Certainly nobody blamed Brady. He led the Patriots on an 11-play, 46-yard drive. He completed 5 of 10 passes. He even scrambled for nine yards.

"I would have loved to pull it off," said Brady. "Every guy in this locker room would have loved to have pulled it off."

Some of the blame was being pointed at the man fighting for his life in the hospital and some of it toward fullback Marc Edwards, who fumbled twice. But as was the case with this team throughout the season, they won as a team and they lost as a team.

Parcells often said, "You are what you are." The Patriots were that. Oh, the effort was there. It wasn't for a lack of trying.

"We kept saying we were better than we were last year, and all of a sudden we're at the end of the season and we had five wins," warned Milloy.

This was a game the Patriots so wanted to win. Forget all of the coaches and players who say that this Patriots-Jets game is "just another game." It's far from it. Certainly the "Border Wars" were over with Parcells' departure from the Jets, but there were still ties. Phifer, Cox, Pleasant, and Otis Smith had all played in New York. Belichick and many of his staff members, including Weis, defensive coordinator Romeo Crennel, defensive backs coach Eric Mangini, and special-teams coach Brad Seely, had coached for the Jets. Belichick's former players—Aaron Glenn, Lewis, Jones, Marcus Coleman, Testaverde, Martin, Chrebet, and so on—were guys he had deep affection for. With all that had happened in the world, maybe the luster of it was gone. But on the field, it was real.

The winning attitude began early. During the preseason at the Patriots' practice field in Foxboro, veteran Anthony Pleasant (No. 98) is helping Brandon Mitchell (No. 99) with technique. In the background is the new CMGI Stadium under construction.

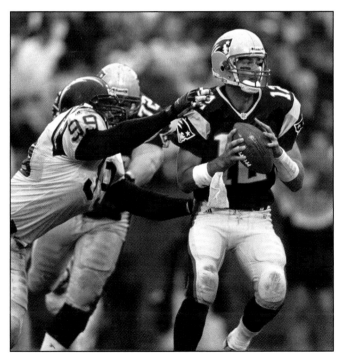

Cool and calm, Tom Brady (No. 12) begins a huge late-game comeback against the San Diego Chargers in an overtime win that turned the Patriots' season around.

Patriotism was at its height following the events of September 11. Here three Patriots fans were really into the red, white, and blue of the Patriots' win over Atlanta.

When Bryan Cox first joined the team in late July he wore No. 0 until he was able to secure the No. 51 he had worn through most of his career. Within days of his arrival, Cox was named a cocaptain. He lived up to the designation, as he was mainly responsible for teaching his teammates how to conduct themselves on and off the field and how to win.

There was no grittier performer than linebacker Tedy Bruschi, who went head over heels to make a play against the athletic St. Louis Ram receivers in a regular-season game on November 18.

The good times for Terry Glenn were few and far between, but he returned from a four-game drug suspension at the start of the season to catch seven passes in an overtime win over the Chargers.

There were many pensive moments for head coach Bill Belichick, but the majority of his decisions were on the money.

Trick plays were a big part of the Patriots' offense. Here, quarterback Tom Brady catches a pass from running back Kevin Faulk in a win over Miami at Foxboro Stadium.

One of Antowain Smith's (No. 32) 12 touchdowns, going over the top of Dolphin cornerback Patrick Surtain (No. 23) in this win over Miami.

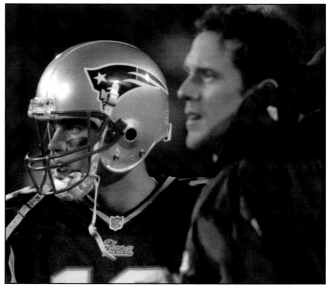

Who would have thought that young Tom Brady would have worn the helmet and veteran Drew Bledsoe would wear the warm-up jacket?

"We've got a lot of games to play and there are signs that we can compete," said Cox. "We just have to look at the film and digest. They ain't gonna cancel the season."

At this point, canceling the season wasn't a bad idea. The Patriots were 0–2, had lost their starting quarterback, and were playing a kid who had thrown three NFL passes. But that was a story that would play out later. Trying to figure out what went wrong in this particular game was the current dilemma, and it really wasn't hard to find the culprits.

One obvious problem was the same thing that plagued the Patriots in the Bengals game: they didn't play a full 60 minutes of football. After battling the Jets tooth and nail to a 3–3 tie at the half, the defense allowed a 93-yard drive in the third quarter, capped by an 8-yard touchdown run by Curtis Martin.

On top of that, the Patriots had four turnovers and committed nine penalties. Was it rust? Was it being too pumped up to play again? Or was it, as Troy Brown would call it, a series of "bonehead plays"?

The first came from the hands of Bledsoe. The veteran quarterback was driving the offense down the length of the field when he tossed an interception to Aaron Glenn at the Jets' 3-yard line with six and a half minutes remaining in the first half and the Patriots leading 3–0.

In the ultimate woulda, coulda, shoulda, it could have been 10–0, and in a game in which the offenses were having problems scoring points, it may have been the difference between winning and losing.

The Jets drove 89 yards, but the Patriots showed the first glimpse of their bend-but-don't-break defense, stopping the Jets and forcing John Hall to boot a 26-yard field goal to make it a 3–3 game.

The Patriots came out of the gate in the third quarter, and Bledsoe again marched them down the field from their own 17 to the Jets' 10. The Patriots were really cranking, chewing up the game clock, and moving the ball.

Then, almost as if the collective heart of the team stopped, Edwards got the call, and as he carried the pigskin, linebacker James

Darling knocked the ball loose from the side, forcing the fumble that the Jets recovered at their own 7-yard line.

"At the one time when it counts, I let a lot of people down," said Edwards.

That's when the Jets drove 93 yards for the go-ahead score. On that drive Bruschi was called for a terrible unnecessary roughness call for slamming into Chrebet from behind after a three-yard gain by fullback Ritchie Anderson on a second-and-10. There was absolutely no need for the hit. But those were the types of problems the Patriots were ironing out early in the season.

Edwards had also miscued with less than three minutes remaining with the Patriots at the Jets' 36 on third-and-7. Bledsoe threw a shovel pass to Edwards, who was stripped of the ball by the talented and ferocious John Abraham, who then recovered the loose ball.

With 9:22 left in the game, Bledsoe hit on a beauty, a 58-yard touch pass to Brown down the right sideline, all the way to the Jets' 11. On third-and-goal from the 8-yard line, Bledsoe threw toward Charles Johnson in the end zone, but the ball got to Jets linebacker James Farrior instead, and he returned it 47 yards to the Jets' 44.

If Bledsoe could speak after this one he would have blamed himself for the loss.

As it was, frustration oozed from the Patriots locker room. Enter Woody telling the *Boston Globe*'s Michael Smith, "You just don't know how upset I am. I'm just trying to hold it in. When we get into the red zone, we've got to convert. That's the bottom line. We can't give up easy points. You work so hard to get all the way down there, and you don't get anything out of it. That's just wasting time."

Two games in the loss column was wasting time, but some Patriots, like Edwards, were filing it in the proper receptacle.

As I approached Edwards the next Wednesday after the game, he bristled when asked about his two fumbles.

"That was over at 3:30 Monday afternoon, bro," he said.

The time referred to the exact time the Patriots had concluded watching the game film of Sunday afternoon's game. Now he was moving on to the next game against the Indianapolis Colts.

Belichick really liked Edwards' skills in this Patriots offense because he became a big-time lead blocker for Antowain Smith and was also used as a quick-hit runner in short situations, a role he performed very well.

The Patriots hadn't had an effective fullback since the Sam Gash–Keith Byars combination in 1996. The Bobby Grier regime signed Tony Carter, but he was not an effective blocker and didn't produce as much in the passing game as the Patriots had hoped. The Patriots didn't re-sign Carter and opted for Edwards, who had a great career at Notre Dame and started out as an effective player for the San Francisco 49ers.

In the first two games, Edwards had gained 44 yards on 10 carries, a lofty 4.4 yards per carry with a long run of 14 yards. He'd caught six passes for 22 yards.

Despite the mistakes, Belichick stuck with him. The coach told the media, when asked if Edwards' playing time would diminish as a result of the miscues, "I don't think so. I think he's still one of our most consistent players. The plays that happened last week . . . you don't want them to happen. I'm not making excuses for him. That play [the shovel pass] wasn't well executed. The fumble [on the run at the Jets' 7]. Again there were a couple of problems on that play. He took a hard hit on the ball and lost it. For the most part, he has been a guy to put the ball on the ground. He hasn't done it his whole career. I would think it wouldn't be a recurring problem."

Edwards had only fumbled three times in his four-year NFL career prior to this season, but two of them came in 2000 with the Browns. What makes that number jump out is that Edwards carried the ball only twice. One of the fumbles he recovered on his own.

"Until we eliminate it, it's a problem," said Belichick.

Edwards was, at one point, talked about being the lone back in a one-back set, but as he said, "When you are a one-back team then whom else are you putting on the field and what does that provide for you? You just don't have time to develop different blocking schemes and that type of thing where you can give the ball to the fullback with the ball real close to the line of scrimmage like that."

Having received that confidence from Belichick, Edwards gave it back to Brady, one of the first endorsements of Brady's ability to replace the injured Bledsoe.

"The team has a lot of confidence in him," said Edwards. "He's learned under Drew; he knows the system. It's a lot different in this situation than it was in Cleveland with Tim Couch where he had to learn things on his own. He didn't have a Drew Bledsoe teaching him the ropes. That has to be a big difference for Tom."

It was a huge win for the Jets, who, according to talented Jets defensive end John Abraham, "wanted to prove to ourselves that we could play. We wanted to show that our defense the first week of the season was a fluke."

The Patriots had scored 20 points in two games, which didn't seem like the type of offense that could come close to beating a jug-gernaut like the Colts, who had followed their rout of the Jets with an equally tremendous offensive output against the Bills, 42–26.

The Colts were averaging 42 points per game.

The Patriots were 0–2.

Now it was time for the Patriots to do what the Jets had already done: prove they could win a tough game in this 2001 season.

CHAPTER 8

Blood, Sweat, and Brady

While Drew Bledsoe was in stable condition at Massachusetts General Hospital, the bleeding in his chest under control, it was up to 24-year-old Brady to stop the bleeding of the 0–2 Patriots.

Brady seemed comfortable as he spoke from the podium in Super Box A at Foxboro Stadium in the usual Wednesday quarterback press conference before the next game. Brady, who later in the season stopped doing the press conferences and spoke only from his locker, showed up with a backpack, looking like a grade-schooler on his way to the bus stop. He was smiling and very excited that he was starting Sunday's game against the Indianapolis Colts.

Wherever his tenure as Patriots quarterback was to lead, he was determined to make it fun. Wide-eyed, he didn't have an inkling of what was ahead, but he was soaking it all in. There was something refreshing about it. Like when your two-year-old sits in front of the TV watching *Barney* or *Sesame Street*, eyes wide open and jaw dropping every time something new or wild or imaginative comes on the screen. That was Brady.

Seeing Brady at the podium was different for the media, which had covered nothing but Bledsoe since his rookie season in 1993. Oh, there were games Bledsoe didn't start when he separated a shoulder or broke a finger, and the backup du jour, Scott Zolak or John Friesz, would get up there and answer questions, but it was different with Brady. This time there were signs Bledsoe wasn't going to play for a long time and Brady was going to be the long-term quarterback.

Sources had told the *Boston Globe* that Bledsoe would miss at least six weeks and maybe more. There was a chance he wouldn't play football again, ever.

Brady certainly appeared ready for anything that was thrown his way. Breaking the ice, he said, "Who wants to shoot?"

He was asked whether playing in front of 80,000 fans in Ann Arbor at the University of Michigan had prepared him for professional football, and he promptly shot back, "It was 112,000." He was then asked if he'd be nervous and he said, "Not a bit, man. Not a bit. I prepare as hard as I can every week. I was ready to start last night if they told me to start last night. I'll be just as ready this week."

The team had a lot of confidence in Brady coming in. Even Belichick said, "I really don't think I'm going to be standing here week after week talking about the problems Tom Brady had. I have confidence in him. I think the team has confidence in him. I think he'll prepare himself and perform at a good level."

Cox wasn't being disrespectful but realistic when he said, "You know there's going to be a drop-off from Drew to Tom. That's not to say Tom's not capable. I think he's very capable. But it's up to the whole team. It's not just up to Tom Brady to fill this void."

Cox was wrong, and he was right.

He was wrong when he said there would be a drop-off. There was none. He was right when he said the rest of the team had to fill the void. It seemed the rest of the team did that. It was quite a team moment really, because they knew collectively if they didn't perform better in all of the areas they'd been lacking in the first two games, the season would be lost. In a way, losing Bledsoe provided the team with a wake-up call: they had to band together.

It was a tough way to have to learn that lesson.

During the week Bledsoe was let out of the hospital, and the first place he went was practice to be with his teammates. He wasn't supposed to do any heavy lifting; he couldn't even lift his kids. But he decided he was going to be on the sideline for the game to offer Brady his support and expertise.

Bruce Armstrong, the six-time All-Pro left tackle, was in town to be inducted in the Patriots Hall of Fame at halftime. It was set up for a good day at the old stadium.

*   *   *

Bryan Cox was a true leader. True leaders lead when the team needs it the most. Cox, commenting on Peyton Manning, said, "I'm going to knock his block off."

Sensing his team needed a boost, Cox provided the Patriots a tremendous jolt on the first series of a game the Patriots had to win. On the Colts' second play of the game, Manning completed a five-yard pass over the middle to Jerome Pathon, who had been one of the stars in the Colts rout of the Buffalo Bills the previous week. Cox came up on Pathon fast and simply laid him out flat. It wasn't Manning, but Pathon would do.

It was a hit heard round sold-out Foxboro Stadium. Cox wound up with 11 tackles, 8 of them solo. But that play set the tone for the game, which the Patriots won, 44–13.

It may have set the tone for the rest of the season.

"Looking back, that hit got the entire team revved up," said fullback Marc Edwards. "It not only got the defense going but the whole team."

It sent a message to the Colts' Big Three of Manning, Marvin Harrison, and Edgerrin James: putting up points at will would (1) not be easy, and (2) be painful.

"You respect your opponent," said Cox, "but at the same time you don't fear your opponent. I played against them the last three years, and I know that we can compete against them. When Bill [Belichick] was in New York as the defensive coordinator, we were the only team to hold them under 20 points in both games [in 1999]. I get paid to do that. For me, it wasn't anything out of the norm for what my job is and what my psyche is. I'm a football player. I appreciate the guys giving me accolades and saying I set the tempo and everything, but I just did my job."

Holding the Colts to 13 points after they'd scored 87 in their first two games was impressive if not remarkable. The 44 points scored by the Patriots were the most by a Patriots team in five years. It was a true testament to Belichick and Crennel, who found ways to get into Manning's head. Until this moment Belichick was 5–13 as the Patriots head coach. That was nothing to do cartwheels over. If at that moment you asked Patriots fans what they thought of giving up a No.1 pick in the 2000 draft (which might have been Seattle's star running back Shaun Alexander) so the Patriots could free Belichick from his New York Jets contract to be the head coach and team figurehead, you wouldn't have got many responses in Belichick's favor.

But then this game happened, and all of the reasons that Bob Kraft did make a commitment to Belichick rang true. Kraft thought that Belichick would be able to game plan against the division's top names, and now he had rendered the superhuman Manning a mere mortal.

Manning had averaged more than 320 yards passing in his first two games, but the Patriots held him to 196 yards. He converted only 5 of 13 third downs. The run stoppers held James to 55 yards on 17 carries and Harrison to three catches for 49 yards.

Belichick has been known to take the strengths of each team and render them impotent. He did it a time or two to Bledsoe when Belichick was the defensive coordinator in New York. Heck, he did it twice during the 1994 season when he was head coach in Cleveland, once in the regular season and again in a wild-card play-off game.

It was the combination of Cox's intimidation, which led to a few dropped balls by Colt receivers who had to be hearing footsteps, and Belichick's mental games with Manning that helped the defense have its best game yet.

With the intensity from guys like Cox, Milloy, Law, Phifer, and Vrabel, the Patriots had a dream day. The secondary forced Manning into three interceptions, and two of them were returned for touchdowns.

"I wasn't really caught off balance," said Manning, who dropped to 0–4 at Foxboro Stadium in his final game there before CMGI Field replaces it. "They rushed three guys most of the time—and dropped back 15 [being sarcastic]. We tried to dink and dunk down the field, make something happen after the catch, but we got some tipped balls and we got behind. It's tough to throw short when you're behind. Either you make the play or you get burned. We got burned most of the time."

Manning, without question the best young quarterback in the game, wasn't sorry to see Foxboro Stadium go. He had lost 29–8 there as a rookie, 31–28 in 1999, and 24–16 in 2000.

"I don't think it's necessarily the place," he said.

Certainly not Peyton's Place.

Nor was it coach Jim Mora's place either. Mora was 0–6 there since 1996.

Otis Smith, the oldest starting cornerback in the NFL, picked off a Manning pass and ran 78 yards to pay dirt for his sixth career touchdown. The interception was pretty in itself: Smith, who was playing the Patriots' familiar Cover-2 defense, slipped out of a double-team, dropped back at the last minute, and made the pick to make it 17–0 Patriots.

Law also ran one back 23 yards.

"I think we're pretty good athletes," said Smith. "People don't think we're superstars like those guys, but we're pretty good athletes and competitive people. To just let guys come in and let them run up and down the field on us, we're not going to let that happen."

Brady's first start was efficient: 13 for 23, 168 yards. He didn't turn the ball over. It was only the second time in the Bledsoe years that a quarterback other than Drew had won a game. The other was Scott Zolak in 1998 versus the San Francisco 49ers.

"I've been preparing for this my whole life," said Brady. "It's not like they pulled me off the street and said, 'You're starting.' I knew eventually this day was going to come since I started playing football."

It was nice to see Bledsoe on the sideline offering support and being a real teammate; at about the same time, outfielder Carl Everett was imploding in the Red Sox clubhouse up the road in Boston. *Globe* columnist Dan Shaughnessy called Bledsoe's nurturing of Brady "very unSox-like."

"I'm ecstatic for Tom," said Bledsoe. "That's really how I expected him to play. He didn't turn the ball over and he made third downs. I was proud of our whole team because they really stepped up."

The only technical assistance Bledsoe offered was about the wind. Bledsoe said, "I knew the wind was a factor, and there were a couple of balls the wind got ahold of. I only told him to keep slinging it, maybe tighten up the spiral in the wind, but that was about it."

Brady was helped by 177 yards rushing (4.5 yards per carry), 94 of them by Antowain Smith, who also had two of the three rushing touchdowns on the day.

Smith touched the ball on 25 of the 62 offensive plays the Patriots ran, and he didn't fumble.

"No turnovers and get the rushing game going, any time you do that you're going to have an advantage. Peyton Manning can't get anything going on the sidelines," said Smith, the veteran running back that used this game as a stepping-stone toward resurrecting his career.

The Patriots had amassed 141 yards on the ground at the half and held the lead.

Smith busted loose for a 39-yard run off beautiful blocks by Woody and Light. "My job," said Woody on the play, "was to hit anybody in my sight. Nothing fancy. Antowain made a cut off my block and he did the rest." He capped off the drive with a four-yard run with 4:23 remaining in the first quarter to give the Patriots a 7–0 lead. A Vinatieri field goal and Smith's touchdown run made it 17–0 before Vinatieri added another three points to give the Patriots a 20–0 half-time lead.

While Cox had set the tone in the first half, Phifer set it in the second half. On the Colts' first possession, Phifer hit the stuffing out of Edgerrin James and forced a fumble recovered by Ted Johnson. Although the Patriots didn't score, the play certainly reinforced who was in charge. On the next series, Phifer picked off a Manning pass that went through Terrell Buckley's hands, and Phifer ran it 15 yards to set up another Vinatieri field goal to make it a 23–0 game.

By the time Manning had begun to solve the riddle, the horse was already out of the barn. He directed a 64-yard drive capped with a 10-yard scamper for a score with 53 seconds remaining in the third quarter to make it a 23–7 game. But that, folks, was as close as it would get.

* * *

Boston Herald columnist Gerry Callahan and *Boston Globe* columnist Bob Ryan had independently referred to Boston as "Loserville," and with good reason. The Celtics and the Bruins were rebuilding, the Patriots had been 5–11 and were starting out lousy, and the Red Sox were in chaos.

But the Indy win seemed to raise the spirits in Loserville.

The Patriots had another divisional foe to prepare for: Miami. The Dolphins are always tough in September and October when the temperatures are still summerlike. Playing in Miami at that time of the year was always a physical and mental challenge.

In Miami Bledsoe would not be around to hold Brady's hand. The veteran quarterback was not cleared by his doctors to fly, and so Brady was on his own but for the support of Huard, who was returning to his old stomping grounds where he once replaced the aging Dan Marino.

The flu wiped out Cox between games. He was walking around the locker room with a towel around his face, hoping not to infect his teammates. He was reminded that when he made an in-studio appearance on CNN during the bye week in 2000, he had said of Dolphins fullback Rob Konrad, "Konrad can't block his way out of a paper bag."

In Miami, Konrad was talking about that outburst with Miami reporters. Konrad said of Cox, "He's going to talk his talk. I don't put that much credibility in what he says. He tries to get his defense fired up. It is what it is. He is what he is, and I'll just leave it at that."

Konrad didn't leave it.

"I can sit here and shoot off about Bryan Cox, about how he's unathletic, he's a marginal football player, all these things, but you know what? That would be unprofessional. He can say what he wants," Konrad continued.

Konrad said when he heard Cox's comments the year before, "It was kind of shocking to me. He was on CNN. I guess they take the person who shoots his mouth off most and put him on television. I played against him after that comment, and I thought I played well. I had a couple of knockdown blocks, and we ran the ball up and down the field on him."

Konrad said of Cox on the field, "He talks all game long. If he played as well as he talked, he'd be a great football player. He talks that well. He talks to everybody."

Even after Konrad's words, Cox didn't back down.

"He can do a lot of things, but when it comes to blocking, I don't think he should get credit because he can't block," said Cox.

It made for a spicier prelude to the Dolphins-Patriots game. Unfortunately, Konrad didn't play because of an injury; on the other hand, Cox, though under the weather, said, "I'd have to be dead not to play."

The teams were coming from different spectrums. The St. Louis Rams had humiliated the Dolphins, 42–10, while the Patriots had beaten the Colts.

The Patriots left Boston for Miami on Saturday afternoon as they usually do. It was hot—the mid-80s.

The United States had performed its first strike against terrorists in Afghanistan, which preempted the broadcast for a while. When the game came back on late in the first quarter, it was obvious the Patriots were playing terribly.

The team that had "turned the corner" against the Colts had walked right into a cement wall called the Miami defense.

They were crushed 30–10.

This, folks, was the lowest moment. This was the valley. They were 1–3, which is even worse than 0–2.

Looking so poised and confident the week before, Brady looked every bit his 24 years with little NFL experience in this one. He completed half of his 24 passes for 86 yards, fumbled twice, and was sacked four times. The Patriots managed only 80 yards rushing as well. The Dolphins acted like caged animals. Not having to cover all of the Rams weapons from the week before, they thought this a walk on the beach.

"We took it personal," said Jurassic defensive end Jason Taylor. "We may not have had a lot of sacks, but stats are for the fans. We had a lot of pressure on Brady."

The Patriots wouldn't admit it but the heat had to be a factor.

"I thought the heat got to them a little bit," said Dolphins quarterback Jay Fiedler. "We had a few long drives that wore on their defense."

You had to blame the heat for Lamar Smith's ripping through the middle of the Patriots defense for 144 yards on 29 carries. Cameras showed the Patriots huffing and puffing and really affected by the heat.

If there had been any hope of the Patriots coming back in this one, it was killed when Brady fumbled a snap at his own 14-yard line late in the third quarter and then watched helplessly as Taylor scooped up the loose ball and ran it in for the touchdown to make it a 27–10 game.

It was evident Brady would not be able to pull the Patriots out of their doldrums in this one, because he couldn't pull himself out first.

"That's the situation we didn't want to put him in," said Woody. "We didn't want him to have to win the game throwing."

Brady spent a long time after the game talking to Milloy about how he didn't like the way the team practiced during the week.

"He pulled me aside and told me this started on Wednesday," said Milloy. "I told him he's a leader, too. He's an honorary captain because he's our quarterback. He can speak up."

Brady was as frank after the game as he's ever been and ever would be for the rest of the season. He said, "I think we've got to take a different approach every day. You shouldn't just get through practice on Wednesday. Get through practice on Thursday. You've got to execute then so you can go out and play great. That's what I'm used to. I missed some throws today. Some throws I'd think I'd make. You miss them in practice, you shouldn't wonder why you miss them in the game."

Obviously someone got to Brady after he spoke those words because he backed off them. For the remainder of his tenure as starting quarterback he spoke only in cliché within the team script.

But the words did make a difference. It brought about more self-reflection from his teammates.

"We got our butt handed to us," said Milloy. "We can't be one-hit wonders. We can't be good one week, collectively as a team, then come out and do what we did today. It's unacceptable."

More than that, at 1–3 it was getting scary.

* * *

The day after, Belichick gathered the team near the practice field and performed a "burying of the ball" ritual to signify that the Dolphins game was now behind them.

"It just seemed like the thing to do," recalled Belichick. "It wasn't planned or anything like that, it just came to me. The players understood what I was doing and they were with me. It was time to just forget about that game and move on to the next one."

CHAPTER 9

Rising in the Fall

It was smack in the middle of fall foliage. Foxboro Stadium was centered in a backdrop of multicolored leaves.

The Patriots were falling for sure. They were 1–3 and gasping for self-respect. Coming off a whooping by the Dolphins they were coming home to face . . . Doug Flutie.

Could the NFL gods have dealt the Patriots a worse hand? Doug Flutie? Boston College's Doug Flutie? The Doug Flutie that was immortalized in this stadium in 1984 with a Hail Mary pass to Gerard Phelan to upset the University of Miami? The Doug Flutie who may be the most popular athlete in Massachusetts's history?

Flutie was now a San Diego Charger, having lost his competition with Rob Johnson in Buffalo. Former Bills GM John Butler, who signed Flutie at age 38 to a nice six-year, $26 million deal, rescued him. Age really didn't matter because Flutie was still a magician, still winning, still pulling rabbits out of hats.

Entering week four against New England, Flutie was 3–1 on the season, 32–15 as a starter. The revitalized Chargers, 1–15 in 2000, led the league in time of possession: 37 minutes, 17 seconds over the first four games.

The Chargers had lost to the Cleveland Browns, 20–16, in week three. With 1:15 remaining in the game the Chargers scored when Tim Couch performed his best magic act yet, finding Kevin Johnson in the end zone to take the lead. Flutie nearly won the game by throwing incomplete passes—Hail Marys—into or toward the end zone. If Curtis Conway had turned the right way on one of them, the Chargers would have come to Foxboro 4–0.

Who would have thought that the Patriots' secret weapon would be Terry Glenn? He had returned from his four-game drug suspension and looked sharp in practice. He was welcomed with open arms by his teammates amid erroneous rumors that they were talking behind his back and didn't want him to return. His teammates were shocked that Glenn could miss most of training camp, all of preseason, and four regular-season games and practices and still be in better shape than most of the players on the field.

Nobody ever said athleticism was a problem for Glenn. He had more of that than the average NFL player. Now if he could just keep himself on one path for an entire NFL season. That was the challenge.

"It's been great just being back on the field and with the guys again," said Glenn. "Everything's been great. It's all about getting back out there and playing football again. It's strange starting this late, but I'm trying my best to get with the rest of the team so I can contribute Sunday."

Glenn was an addition the Patriots passing game sorely needed. Brady needed weapons, someone to get open. Glenn was very confident he could "make the offense better."

Another amazing addition was Andruzzi. He had sprained his left knee against the Dolphins. Listed as "out" on the injury report earlier in the week, the Patriots upgraded him to "doubtful," which meant there was a 25 percent chance he'd play. Well, he played.

"I got treatment through the week and it kept getting better and better," said Andruzzi. "I'm not a receiver or a quarterback or a running back. At my position, if I can stand, I'll play."

In one of the gutsiest performances you'll ever see, Andruzzi played all the plays, and, though his knee hurt and throbbed, he hung in there and absorbed the pain.

Defensively, besides obvious survival, pride was at stake. The Patriots defense had been outmuscled, plain and simple, against Miami.

"It's not really what they're doing, it's what we're not doing," said Hamilton. "When it comes to stopping the run, you've got to have attitude. Attitude doing what you're supposed to be doing, the right technique and being in the gap you're supposed to be in."

The Patriots had been tackling horribly over the first four games, but they could not afford to do that against tough rookie runner LaDainian Tomlinson and especially not against Flutie when he scrambled. The Patriots were 25th in the NFL rankings against the run after four games.

Brady needed to show Patriots Nation he could rebound from a poor performance in Miami and get the team headed on the right track.

All of these factors were converging on one extremely important day at Foxboro Stadium, where Flutie was 12–1.

* * *

The *S* word started to surface after the Patriots pulled out a stunning 29–26 overtime victory over Flutie and the Chargers on October 14. *Special* was the word being used to describe Brady.

"If he keeps playing like this over the next four or five games, his value is going to go through the roof," said an NFL scout who was at the game. "He's a tough kid with excellent poise. To pick up blitzes and make something happen, and hang in the pocket like he does, is worth a lot. The Patriots are eventually going to have a tough call. Obviously Drew is their guy, but how long do you keep Brady on the bench?"

Brady, 15 years his junior, had really beaten Flutie at his own game: comebacks and miracle finishes.

Speculation during the week was that if the Chargers had a comfortable lead, the crowd would cheer for Flutie and turn this into a danged home game. But it never got to that point.

With 8:38 remaining in regulation and the team in real danger of going 1–4 and probably kissing the season away, Brady and the Patriots trailed by 10 points, 26–16. What was to come was remarkable: three scores in their next three possessions, ending with Vinatieri's 44-yard field goal in overtime to win it.

"Tom Brady came in and played the game of his life," said veteran Charger linebacker Junior Seau. "We couldn't get them off the field. He just played an exceptional game and made the plays when they needed to be made."

Weis' game plan featured Brady all the way. Antowain Smith was in cobwebs for this one. He averaged 1.2 yards per carry.

"When we played Indianapolis we were able to run the ball," said Brady. "The game plan was to come out firing." He fired 54 times and completed 33. He threw no interceptions and two touchdowns. He threw for 364 yards, 130 of them coming in the final three possessions. He accounted for 13 points in 13 minutes.

This wasn't quite as great as Bledsoe's incredible performance to lead the Patriots back against the Vikings, which saved the 1994 season and began a string of seven straight wins to the playoffs. But this one had to rank right up there, especially considering Brady was starting only his third NFL game.

Seven of those fifty-four passes were thrown to Glenn for 110 yards and one touchdown. The troubled receiver was carefree, making tough catches and acting as if he'd never missed a beat.

Even Glenn chimed in on his new quarterback: "I like his attitude. It's a real good attitude for the position, and it's the right attitude for the type of receivers we have."

Huard said it best with his comments: "Tom put himself on the map today. He was calm, cool, and collected. He wore the same face he wore the entire game."

This victory, which raised the record to 2–3, was all about deter-mination and the old cliché of never giving up. Heck, the entire sea-son was a cliché that most of us kept missing. This one was hard to miss, although the fans who were heading for the parking lot were missing it.

The comeback wasn't a panicked one. It was almost methodi-cal. The first drive went 69 yards on 15 plays. Nobody was hurry-ing; everyone was businesslike. Brady went five for eight. Smith, who had only 36 yards on the day, amassed 19 of them on the drive. Big runs were what Smith was all about, and none was big-ger than five yards on a fourth-and-2 from the Patriots' 48-yard line to extend the drive.

Brady calmly fired medium-range passes. Thirteen yards to Glenn. Twelve yards to Kevin Faulk. Ten yards to Troy Brown. The Patriots got all the way to the 3-yard line. The Patriots could have gone for it on fourth-and-goal, but Belichick knew there was plenty of time and brought Vinatieri out to kick the 23-yard gimme.

Now it was a one-touchdown game, 26–19.

The Patriots defense was certainly the underrated aspect of the win. Despite the fact that the Chargers had scored 26 points, the Patriots defense had held Tomlinson to 65 yards on 21 carries at that point in the game. No other team had contained him that well.

In this intense game, one that required all of the energy in a per-son's body, Belichick asked his defense for another stop. This was truly a test. What is memorable here is that Tomlinson gained eight yards on first down, but the Chargers went three-and-out. That's right. On second down, Ted Johnson, with help from Hamilton, came up and made a big play, holding Tomlinson to a yard. On third down, Cox and McGinest stopped him for no gain.

Now that's defense.

There was 2:10 remaining when the Patriots started their next drive at their own 40. Brown had had one of his many clutch moments of the season when he returned the ensuing punt 40 yards to midfield, but he was knocked back 10 yards on a holding call on Terrance Shaw.

"Not one time did I doubt that we were going to go down the field and score," said Patten, who caught seven passes that day.

Confidence was building in young Tom. The players believed in him.

Brady was now being asked to give the Patriots life so they could send it into OT. Out of the shotgun, the young gunslinger went five for eight again. The big plays were a 16-yard pass to Brown, who legged it most of the way; a beautifully thrown 26-yard bullet down the field between a pair of defenders to Patten; and rat-a-tat-tat, a three-yard TD pass to a wide-open Wiggins in the end zone with 40 seconds left on the clock. Good timing for Wiggins because Belichick had criticized his tight ends during the pregame for not getting open. Following Vinatieri's kick, the Patriots had tied the Chargers 26–26.

"The defense knows you're throwing, you know you're throwing, and you've just got to get the communication going," said Brady. "The two-minute drill really puts the pressure on the secondary. It got to the point in the game where we had to move the ball quickly, and guys were getting open for me."

Flutie, 20 of 32 for 270 yards, still had 31 seconds following the kickoff. Starting at the 23, Tomlinson busted out for 14 yards, and Flutie hit Curtis Conway for 24 more. After a spike, the Chargers trotted out field-goal kicker Wade Richey. But the 59-yard attempt fell about five yards short, and it was off to overtime.

The Chargers won the OT toss and elected to receive. This gave Flutie yet another chance to beat the Patriots in miraculous fashion. But it wasn't meant to be. They went three-and-out and punted.

The Patriots started the winning drive at the 23-yard line.

The big play was a 37-yard penalty on Chargers' cornerback Alex Molden, who held Patten down the field. It was interesting because Brady audibled when he saw the Chargers were showing blitz.

"We talked during the week that if they ran a certain blitz, we'd audible out. David fought for the ball, which drew the call. The important thing is we executed what we practiced," explained Brady.

Brady actually underthrew Patten, who had to come back for the ball. That's what caused Molden to grab him. Molden said the flag surprised him and he thought the crowd influenced the referee's call. "You play on the road, they get the crowd into it, hooting and hollering and wanting a flag," said Molden.

Afterward, Belichick relayed what he had told Brady: "The main thing I wanted to get across to Tom was to just give us a chance. Don't overthrow it. Just give our receiver a chance to make a play on the ball, and he certainly did that on that one."

The important thing was that the ball was at the Chargers' 32.

After three short completions by Brady, the ball sat at the 26. The field was wet and slightly muddy. On third down, Belichick called for Vinatieri, who in the first half had missed an extra point that might have avoided the extra period.

Vinatieri made the kick. The crowd went wild.

"[Inside linebacker coach] Pepper Johnson told me after the miss, 'It's gonna come back to you.' And he was right," Vinatieri said. "I couldn't have had a worse spot on the field, but the snap and hold were clean and I was able to get it through."

The final three plays didn't tell all of the interesting aspects of this game.

The Patriots had led 9–6 at the half, as Vinatieri had hit a 26-yard field goal and Brady had connected with Glenn on a 26-yard touchdown pass—Brady's first NFL touchdown pass, a beauty thrown perfectly between two defenders.

The Patriots, who had been outscored 51–10 in the third quarter through five games, squandered the lead when Flutie hit Conway down the field for 56 yards and 19 yards, while Tomlinson capped off the drive with a one-yard run that made it a 13–9 Chargers game.

The Patriots retook the lead on Smith's one-yard run capping a 71-yard drive to make it 16–13 Patriots, but the Chargers regained the lead with 10 minutes left in the game, when Flutie found tight end Steve Heiden for a three-yard touchdown pass and a 19–16 advantage.

Enter Lee Johnson.

Unfortunately his play wound up being his exit. The 39-year-old punter, who held NFL records for most punts and most punting yardage and who held the distinction of being the player who had lost more games than any player in NFL history, summed up his play this way: "I murdered us."

Well, not quite. In fact, his play may have inspired the Patriots.

Johnson wasn't punting well, really. He was getting great rolls that helped the gross average, but his hang time was lacking. He had kicked a liner to Tim Dwight, which Dwight returned 26 yards to the Patriots' 34 to set up the Chargers go-ahead touchdown. Earlier he had shanked a 30-yarder.

But *the* play was really bad.

At the Patriots' 11, Johnson was back in punt formation when Charger Derrick Harris faked 21-year-old rookie Hakim Akbar out of his shoes on the left side and came in on Johnson clean. Johnson, who had been in the league for 17 years and had seen everything, apparently hadn't seen this. He brought his left leg up as if to begin the punting motion but "I saw I couldn't get the ball off. At least I felt I couldn't have got the ball off. Could I have?"

Probably not.

But he took the ball and placed it in his left hand and raised it. It looked as if he was trying to keep it away from Harris. Johnson described it this way: "I was doing a ballet. When he spun me around, I realized I wasn't going to kick the ball."

"I saw him holding the ball awkwardly, so I tackled him," said Harris. The ball squirted loose and Harris picked it up and ran six yards for a touchdown.

The play didn't amuse Belichick. He said of Vinatieri's missed extra point and Johnson's faux pas, "The whole kicking game was just terrible, just terrible. We are not good enough to create that many opportunities for our opponents in the kicking game. We just can't do that. It has been a strength for us, really, but that was the worst we've played in the kicking game in a year and a half I've been here and we just can't go on like that."

Without actually saying it, he pretty much fired Johnson on the spot. The only question was how long would it take the Patriots to find a new punter? On Monday, October 16, Johnson was called into Belichick's office and told he was gone.

"It happens to every player sooner or later," said Johnson after hearing the news. "Those aren't the things you remember. As long as I've played, there are a lot of memories of positive things that will stick."

At the time, Johnson, who was a successful day trader in the stock market, felt he had punted for the last time.

"I don't think anyone will pick me up at this point," said Johnson. "The age, the way I'm kicking, I'm just off. Bad timing. I'm just off."

Johnson, a very smart, personable guy, felt he was off because he was flustered in training camp when Belichick brought punters Brad Costello and Dan Hadenfeldt in to compete with Johnson. While some players enjoy competition, Johnson felt that this far into his career he had to worry about getting ready for the season at his own pace rather than worry about the challenge of some young kid.

Johnson ended up hooking on with the Minnesota Vikings, signing a deal for the remainder of the season on December 12, 2001.

For the Patriots, Ken Walter, who had punted in Carolina and had some problems there before being released after last season, was the chosen one. Walter became the anti-Johnson—great hang time, few returns against him, and one of the best net averages in the league.

"I really don't think the performance is going to be worse than what it's been," said Belichick.

It was one of the little personnel decisions that Belichick made along the way that proved golden. Now 2–3 and climbing back into in the AFC East, the Patriots looked for the elusive .500 mark.

CHAPTER 10

A Developing Story

Hard to say with a record of 2–3 whether the Patriots were on to something. This much was clear: they were developing three very good young players—a quarterback, a left tackle, and a defensive tackle. All in one year. That's pretty impressive.

The quarterback of course was Brady. The left tackle was Light. The defensive tackle was Seymour.

Belichick probably had to catch himself with praise of these guys at this stage, only five games into the season. He said of Brady after speaking glowingly of him following the San Diego game, "Wait a minute, let me just clear that up. It's way too early to retire his number or anything like that. I thought he played well in the game. I thought he brought the team back from a deficit in the fourth quarter and made a couple of plays. We're 2–3 and we haven't won a game on the road. He's played a couple of good games. But I think it's way too early to put him in the Hall of Fame."

Not that anyone was, really; it's just that the gushing over Brady had begun, some of it with good reason.

"Let's wait until we beat somebody on the road, win a divisional game, and have a little better record. I think we're a long way off from the 1980 Chargers, averaging 550 yards per game. I don't think we're gonna throw it 54 times. A balanced offense is our best thing."

On Light, the coach was again cautious.

"Matt's making progress," admitted Belichick. "Improving. He's done a better job in the running game. Pass protection against a good speed rusher is a challenge. He's held up OK. Each week there's going to be a good player out there. He's one of those guys who need to keep producing and keep going. Be more consistent, and he'll be OK. But I don't think we're quite there yet."

Belichick was right about speed rushers giving Light problems. Jason Taylor was tough against him, but Light really held his own against the bigger, bulkier guys like the Colts' Chad Bratzke, whom he was about to face again at the RCA Dome in Indianapolis on Sunday, October 21.

As for Seymour, he was not only playing a new position—nose tackle—but also playing it well. The pocket was collapsing. Some teams were double-teaming him, and he'd still get good movement upfield.

He was a nice, mild kid off the field. On it he was as ferocious as could be.

After five games, the Patriots definitely had some outstanding young players. The true test would be how they performed for 16 games. They got their answer on that too, and it was thumbs-up on all three.

Meanwhile, Bledsoe's health was improving, and he was cleared for light jogging. For the first time he was listed as "doubtful" instead of "out" on the injury report. After a week's worth of speculation, Bledsoe was not the third or emergency quarterback but was holding the clipboard on the sideline with a headset on.

At this stage, Bledsoe was still feeling this was his team. He told Borges, "I feel I'll be the starter for as long as I'm here. But at the same time, it's just not given to somebody [the No. 1 job]. I feel the situation is clear to me and to Tom how it works, but as long as we're here, I'd expect him to push me for my spot. Tom is probably the best guy who's been behind me here. No discredit to Zo

[Scott Zolak] or John Friesz, but he's a guy who'll drive me to continue to progress."

Bledsoe was also not upset that Brady was definitely emerging as the fans' choice. The problem was, in many cases, that those who cherished Brady ripped Bledsoe apart.

"Of Tom's fans," Bledsoe told Borges, "I'm at the top of the list. He's played very well. I wouldn't take anything away from him. He's played the way I expected."

Belichick was certainly into the stage where he was being asked, "Does Drew get his job back when he returns?"

Belichick had the answer down pat: "When Drew is back at 100 percent, we'll deal with that then. But we're a long way from that now. The next step is for Drew to resume moderate to heavy physical activity to regaining his skills at his position and being the third quarterback. Until they happen, it's way premature to talk about anything else."

Also during this week, legendary sports-talk-show caller "Butch from the Cape" lost a long battle with cancer. A Yankees fan, Butch had long been a critic of the Boston sports scene and even referred to Bledsoe as "Nancy Drew." As Bill Griffith wrote in his TV column in the *Globe* on October 18, "When they open the Talk Show Hall of Fame, he'll be the charter member in the Caller Division, and of course, he'll go in as a unanimous selection. He was the Howard Cosell of his genre."

The bad news on the field that week was that, after having caught seven passes in the San Diego game, Glenn injured his left hamstring in practice on October 18. He had come up lame halfway through the afternoon practice after making a sharp cut on a pass route.

Asked the severity of it, Belichick said, "It wasn't a 911 emergency."

Glenn was out, even though up until the walk-through on Saturday he had said, "It doesn't feel that bad right now. It feels better than it did on Thursday." But while Glenn was warming up pregame on Sunday, it took a turn for the worse.

Glenn said he had warned the coaching staff that his legs were hurting prior to pulling the hamstring on Wednesday in practice. He claimed that he was asked to run several go patterns anyway. Glenn's agent, Jim Gould, was miffed over this, saying, "The gloves are off. If they want to ruin Terry's career, they're going to have to go through me. I'm sick of it. Even after their actions he did everything he could to play. It's unconscionable. If they want to fight, we'll fight."

Glenn wouldn't play again until December 9 versus Cleveland.

*　　*　　*

October 21 was a good day and a sad one as well.

The Patriots beat the living tar out of the Indianapolis Colts, 38–17, in their own indoor yard, reaching the coveted .500 mark and winning their first road game. The Patriots had lost 14 of their last 16 road games before this win.

It was the first major sign of Weis' imagination and genius. Oh sure, back in the first Colts game he had Brady throw a seven-yard pass to Cox. There were a few reverses here and there, but those were minor league compared to the stuff he had going for this one.

Bledsoe, who was on the sideline, said afterward, "That was one of the greatest game plans I've ever seen."

The sad part was that the Colts had played the Patriots as a divisional opponent for the final time. With all of the clout Kraft had around the league, even he couldn't stop this realignment stuff. Indy would no longer be in the Patriots' division.

For a team that was supposed to be the favored winner in the AFC East and possibly the Super Bowl, the Colts were awful. You'd think there'd be something brewing inside Mora's gang that wanted revenge for the pounding they took in Foxboro in week three. There was none of that. The Patriots took the wind out of their sails immediately, blocking two field goals—one by Brandon Mitchell and one by Tebucky Jones—in the first 30 minutes of the game.

The real story was Patten, an ex–Arena League guy who was lugging around sacks of coffee beans when he was out of football three years prior. On this day he accounted for four touchdowns. He ran for one touchdown, caught two, and passed for one.

Basically it was football's version of the cycle.

Weis said, "I can't remember a game with three one-play drives. I told Brady, 'Don't apologize for scoring fast.' Nobody can complain about that kind of production. We had thrown 20 tosses [to Antowain Smith] in the first game, so what am I going to do, repeat that? We had to do something different."

In the first quarter Patten took a handoff from Antowain Smith, who had started to run left while Patten was heading right. Patten went 29 yards down the right side for a touchdown.

The most memorable trick play came in the second quarter. Here, Brady took the snap and then passed, or lateraled, to Patten on the left side. It appeared like just another wide receiver screen pass until Patten shocked everyone by heaving the ball downfield to Troy Brown, who took it 60 yards for the score.

"That was one of those plays we practiced on Thursday and Friday and we did on Sunday," recalled Weis. "At first we had Terry [Glenn] throwing it, and then we had Troy, and then David Patten looked up at me and said, 'What about me, I can throw it.' He kept bugging me about throwing, so finally I let him do it. When we knew Terry wasn't going to be able to play in the game, we decided Patten was going to throw to Troy."

Brady remembers thinking, "Jeez, Charlie's going crazy again."

It was crazy, but Weis was setting a trend around the league. As teams began to watch the Patriots on offense, suddenly more gadget plays were popping up.

"If you don't have tons of firepower and you don't have a ton of weapons. . . . I mean you can dink and dunk, but you know, we have good receivers and a quarterback and you just have to try things," said Weis.

Colts booter Mike Vanderjagt made a field goal from 42 yards with 5:44 remaining in the first quarter. But with the Patriots starting their next drive at the 9-yard line, Weis took another shot. This time Brady delivered a perfect ball as Patten beat Dave Macklin on a post pattern and went 91 yards, the longest play from scrimmage in Patriots history.

"If you feel you have a chance to put a fork in somebody, go for the jugular. We had them reeling," said Weis.

Weis often practices trick plays with his players.

"I think we look forward to practice to see what Charlie is gonna come up with next," said Patten. "I think it helps guys stay focused. I really do. It's not the same old stuff. It keeps guys perked up."

Weis, asked after the season how many trick plays he had, responded, "Plenty."

"Listen, we draw them up in the dirt just like you do," said Weis, about how he gets the ideas for the plays. "Bill and I get together and say this guy does this and this guy does that. . . . You have to know your personnel and see if you have a guy who can pull off whatever part of the play needs to be done. If you feel you have the people, then you practice it. If it works successfully in practice, you think about a situation in the game where you can pull it off. What people don't understand is, we study what the other team's defense is doing and analyze what situation we feel we might best be able to utilize it. It's not just throw it out there and see what happens."

Weis has plays in his repertoire and in his mind that we have never seen, and maybe we'll never see them. He uses them at a point in the game when he wants to seize some type of opportunity, whether it's to put the final nail in the coffin of an opponent or to get something going with the offense or to show the opponent that they need to be wary of more than just short passes and Smith running a toss.

Weis is a jovial guy but one who knows his stuff. In his first tenure with the Patriots under Parcells as a position coach, he had quite the track record. In 1994 he coached Ben Coates. Result: 96 catches, the all-time record for catches in a season by a tight end. In 1995 he coached Curtis Martin. Result: 1,487 yards rushing, the Patriots' all-time single-season record. In 1996 he coached receivers. Result: Glenn with 90 receptions, an NFL rookie record.

He is the master at understanding what his players can or can't do.
"You can't force a player to do something he can't do or doesn't want to do. It won't work," said Weis. "The player has to be comfortable with the call. If you make a QB do what he can't do you might have a fumble or an interception or a turnover that could mean the difference between winning and losing a game."

That's one reason Brady succeeded so well in 2001. Weis was a master of working with his players, calling plays they were comfortable running.

Weis recalled from his days with the Jets in 1998, "We'd throw out 10–15 plays a week," said Weis. "If Vinny didn't feel comfortable with it, it was gone, because if you run it, something bad always happens."

Weis knows he can call the most creative plays in the world, but if each unit isn't taking care of business it will all break down, and if the quarterback doesn't believe in the play it won't be executed properly.

But it wasn't all offense in this game. Ted Johnson, whose playing time had diminished, made a huge hit on Edgerrin James, forcing a fumble that was recovered by Bruschi at the Colts' 24 with 3:53 remaining in the half. Brady handed off to Edwards for 10 yards, then Brady took to the air. He flared one out to Wiggins in the end zone for two yards, giving the Patriots a 28–3 lead.

The Colts settled for another field goal before the end of the half and trailed at the break, 28–6. As usual, the Patriots had a letdown to start the third quarter when Manning, who still led the Colts to 484 yards of offense in defeat, moved 68 yards before capping the drive with a two-yard TD pass to Marvin Harrison, followed by a two-point conversion toss to tight end Ken Dilger.

It was a two-touchdown game, not the safest of margins against the Colts.

Belichick asked for more, and he received it.

The teams actually exchanged field goals before a late third-quarter drive sealed the win. That drive was helped when Brown drew a 38-yard interference penalty on Macklin, who continued to have one of the worst days in cornerback history.

Brady found Patten for a six-yard catch in the end zone, making it 38–17. It was Brady's sixth touchdown pass and ninth score in his last 12 series. Then in the fourth quarter, the Patriots kept the Colts off the field for 10:11. The Colts defense couldn't make a play to save its life.

Lost in all the trickery was Brady's excellent game. He enjoyed a quarterback rating of 148.3, completing 16 for 20 for 202 yards. He extended his streak of throwing no interceptions at the start of his career to 131.

"I still haven't proven anything," said Brady. "It's only four games, but it's a good start, winning on the road and taking the crowd out of the game."

Brady was now becoming a superstar. His agent, Donald Yee, was getting a feel for what was happening. He began receiving many calls for Brady to do endorsements, but Yee was trying to harness the temptation.

Yee said, "We don't want Tom spread thin. If he's out making appearances, making commercials, and spending time on photo shoots, he's not resting. He understands that. If he keeps going, Tom will make his money. But you have to establish yourself as a football player first."

Asked how Brady lasted so long in the draft in 2000, Yee said, "A lot of scouts committed scouting malpractice letting Tom go that late."

The guy who hit it straight on was Rehbein. Belichick had told Rehbein in 2000 that with his quarterbacks getting up in age, he wanted to draft one. Rehbein narrowed it to two: he chose Brady.

Kraft was staying way out of the quarterback controversy. Asked about it he said, "Those are good problems. I wish we had more of those problems."

Right now it was no problem at all. The Patriots were at .500, moving on to Denver, which would continue to be their house of horrors.

CHAPTER 11

The Glenn Files

Ending months of the most turbulent times involving one player in Patriots history, Terry Glenn was dealt to the Green Bay Packers on March 8, 2002, for a fourth-round pick and a conditional pick in 2003.

Oh, Irving Fryar had been bad in his time with the Patriots in the eighties, but never had one player been so the subject of negativity from the start of training camp until this moment. Dubbed Terry "Oil Can" Glenn by *Globe* columnist Dan Shaughnessy (referring to Dennis "Oil Can" Boyd, who had a troubled existence with the Red Sox in the mideighties), Glenn made only one significant contribution: seven catches against San Diego.

Glenn's season was a washout, beset with personal problems, three suspensions (which included the playoffs and the Super Bowl), and a questionable hamstring injury.

Glenn's personal demons had caught up with him.

Having witnessed the murder of his mother when he was 13 years old, he was always a troubled kid. It's been easy for people to say over the years that he should "get over it." While some of his teammates also had hard-luck stories in their childhoods, nothing could top the severity of Glenn's.

In the six years I've known Glenn, I have come to realize that (1) he was not the evil guy so many thought and (2) he definitely had a different thought process than most.

When your job is to write about major sports teams, the players tend to blend together after a while. Except for the great ones, there are few distinguishing marks. Glenn stuck out.

I considered myself fortunate to be able to get the inside story on Glenn, perhaps the most enigmatic figure in Boston sports history. The team didn't like it when I presented Glenn's side of the story, but reporters are supposed to be fair and tell both sides. That's what I did.

While he was AWOL from Patriots training camp after learning the news he would serve a four-game suspension for violating the NFL's substance policy, I phoned him in Columbus, Ohio, and he asked me, "What do you think I should do?" At the time it was obvious what he should do: he needed to get back to camp so Gould could at least sit with Wasynczuk and Belichick and come up with some resolution. He also needed to get back to Smithfield, Rhode Island, so the Patriots wouldn't threaten to place him on the reserve/suspended list, which would have meant he'd be gone for all of 2001 and the first four games of 2002.

As it turned out, the Patriots placed him on the list the day after Glenn, along with his agent, had decided to return to camp. I know this because I spoke to Glenn the evening of August 13. He said he was planning to return on August 14.

Gould had phoned Wasynczuk the day of August 13 to inform him he was bringing Glenn back East for a meeting. Wasynczuk got back to him later and informed Gould he needn't bother because Glenn was being placed on the reserve/suspended list.

Arbitrator Richard Bloch, who heard the 13-hour expedited case on September 6 at Foxboro Stadium, ruled two days after the September 11 events that the Patriots should have allowed Glenn to return to the team in a reasonable amount of time. If the Patriots were going to place Glenn on the list, they should have done it five days after they'd sent a warning letter to Glenn. The Patriots reasoned that they gave Glenn a chance to return but that they had simply reached their breaking point. Bloch rescinded the reserve/left-camp list designation, which meant Glenn would have to serve only his four-game drug suspension.

Glenn's problems with Belichick had started way before camp, however. Belichick fumed that Glenn didn't take part in the off-season conditioning program, while the rest of the team seemed to bond during this process. Glenn had always said he wanted to stay home in Columbus so he could be close to his son, Terry Jr.

"In Terry's case, his presence wasn't felt here. He hasn't been part of hardly anything we've done in the off-season," said Belichick.

On May 15, Walpole, Massachusetts, police answered a call placed by an anonymous caller indicating a domestic struggle at Glenn's townhouse. When police arrived, they arrested Glenn and charged him with assault and battery and intimidation of a witness. The woman he allegedly assaulted was Kimberly Combs, the mother of his child.

Glenn had certainly had his share of troubles, but inflicting harm on a woman? This had wandered into an entirely different realm.

After the incident, Glenn did not speak to Belichick or anyone in the Patriots organization about the matter. Glenn claimed he was heading to Foxboro Stadium to meet with Belichick, but he had media tailing him. He then decided he would head back to his Walpole home and drive to Columbus, Ohio.

On July 20, Norfolk County, Massachusetts, prosecutors released an eyewitness account by five-year-old Terry Jr. who said, "Daddy pushed Mommy. Daddy took the phone from Mommy's ear and took it out of the wall." The prosecutors, however, couldn't base their case on Terry Jr.'s testimony.

It wasn't until January of 2002 that Glenn was cleared of all charges. Combs, who had originally told police Glenn had been abusive toward her that night and at other times, recanted her story. The prosecutors could not go forth with the case without her testimony.

The Patriots didn't say much about the domestic situation, nor did they back Glenn. Comparing it to Baltimore Ravens middle linebacker Ray Lewis' double-murder charge in Atlanta two off-seasons ago at which time the Ravens supported Lewis' claim of innocence, Belichick said, "Ray Lewis was at the Baltimore facility every single day last year during the off-season."

Shot back Gould: "Well, maybe if the Patriots had supported Terry like the Ravens supported Lewis, Terry would have been there as well."

The Patriots had received word during this time that Glenn had violated his drug policy, and they decided to withhold a $1 million payment on his staggered $11.5 million signing bonus, which was scheduled to be distributed in 26 payments.

The Patriots basically advised Glenn not to show up at the June minicamp because they wanted him to "take care of business." Belichick didn't want the distraction because he felt it was a very important camp.

By the time training camp rolled around, Glenn was there, but in early practices he was out with the second and third units. Belichick was rewarding the players who had attended the off-season program and had participated in the June minicamp.

This didn't sit well with Glenn.

Amid his anger, he made the practice catch of the camp, an outstretched sideline grab of a Brady throw. It was an eye-opener, one that proved beyond a reasonable doubt that he was one of the most physically talented receivers in the game. Even his teammates and coaches applauded.

It was perhaps the last time he would hear cheers.

On August 3, a hot afternoon in Smithfield, Rhode Island, the NFL's decision came down. Gone for four games. Glenn got the news from Belichick and hopped into his Land Rover. Upon leaving, an angry Glenn made a few comments caught by former *MetroWest Daily News* reporter (now of the *Providence Journal*) Tom E. Curran.

Glenn said, "Somebody did something. Somebody called somebody, and now I don't know what's going on. They've been trying to get rid of me for two years. I don't know why they even re-signed me if they don't want me around."

Those words did not help his cause with the Patriots. They angered Patriots management and ownership.

A week went by. Glenn did not speak to anyone except Gould.

Right before the Patriots' first preseason game, against the New York Giants at Foxboro Stadium on August 10, Glenn returned a call to this reporter. Asked what was going on, he responded as he usually does: "Just chillin'."

I asked Glenn for an interview, to which he responded, "You got a game to cover, don't you? Listen, I'll talk to you later and you can ask me anything. Call me at halftime so I know what's going on in the game."

"Ah, Terry, listen, I can still cover the game and talk to you . . ."

Quite frankly, in more than 20 years of covering sports in Boston, I had never come across an athlete who knew anything about deadlines or understood I had to concentrate on the game rather than talk to him.

"Don't worry, we'll hook up later, man," he said.

Feeling as though I'd spoken to Glenn for the last time, I reluctantly hung up. At halftime, I called him back and, much to my surprise, he answered.

"How did the receivers do?" Glenn asked. "I like Patten. He can really play. Charles [Johnson] is a real pro and Torrance can really catch the ball. OK, call me after the game. Call me after you get home."

After filing my story and driving 40 minutes to my home, I phoned Glenn. No answer. It was about 1:30 A.M. at this point—too late to get something in the paper even if I had talked to him. I stayed awake for a while, waiting to see if he'd call back. At about 2:00 A.M., Glenn called back.

"Why don't we meet in person tomorrow and I'll answer your questions?"

Rather than agree, I started asking my questions. I asked, he answered. It kept going until I had an interview. It was 3:00 A.M. and nothing to do but hold it a day. The story appeared in the Sunday *Globe*, top of the page.

It was a long interview with a lot of information to chew. The highlights:

"When I heard the news . . . it's something I never thought would happen to me," said Glenn. "Football is my whole life. It means a lot more to me than anyone else, because other players have something else. I have nothing. I have nothing else.

"I have money, but what I've found is money for someone like me isn't always the best thing. I don't play the game for money. Playing football allows me to feel alive. You see, I don't have any family members here. I don't have a mother or a father or aunts or uncles. I have my little sister but she's in college. They [the NFL] took away my life and I was upset. I was upset because this shouldn't have happened.

"I know it's not my fault. Believe me, I understand the drug policy. I've been living it for three years. Three times a week I get tested. I missed one test and I was warned about it. So I'm aware of every step I have to follow in this program."

Glenn said he went to visit a participant in the Texas Relays (track meet) in the off-season, but he claims he attempted to call his medical adviser to tell him of his whereabouts.

"I have documented evidence," said Glenn. "I have phone records. My lawyers presented them at the appeal. It was a cut-and-dried case. The Players' Association thought so, too. I told them [medical advisers] where I was, so if they wanted to send someone to Texas to test me, fine. I didn't receive a callback from them until two days later. Two days later! And then I took the test and it was negative."

He admitted to me he entered the drug program because he had "tried some marijuana [at a party]. It was a mistake because I don't do drugs. But I paid the price for that mistake. I'm not blaming anyone but myself for that. I took the penalty, went into the program, and did everything they wanted me to do."

Glenn spoke of the constant drug tests he was forced to take: "Once you're in the program your life isn't your own. It's always in the back of your mind; you're going to get tested. So I was conscious of it. I understood it. In this case, there was miscommunication on *their* part, not mine, and because of it my football career is being taken away."

He didn't feel the team supported him in his domestic-abuse case.

"I don't want to be wrapped up in a little blanket like a baby and cuddled," said Glenn. "I just want the team to offer some support for a player they supposedly feel is one of their best. If I'm that big of a burden, don't keep me here."

He said he'd never used his childhood as an excuse for his problems.

"I've never used my childhood as an excuse for anything," said Glenn. "Other people have said that. I'm responsible for what I do, act, and say. And really, it doesn't matter how other people handle it. Every person is different and handles things in their own way."

He said he'd given thought to just walking away from football.

"I've thought about it seriously," said Glenn. "I've done good things with my money. I live pretty low key. I mean I never go out of my house. I sit here sometimes and there are media people ringing my doorbell and cameras on my lawn. They wait until I pull out and they're following me places. I don't know if I want that all the time.

"Believe me, I know I'm in the prime of my career. I know when I step on the field I can change a game, and that gives me the best feeling that I know."

The story received national play. The Patriots were flabbergasted.

During his holdout, Gould made comments to ESPN that he had advised Glenn to return to camp so he could do something for him. Glenn heard the interview, and for a day or two he was angry with Gould, feeling even his agent was hanging him out to dry. But Glenn eventually came to his senses and realized Gould was right. The two spoke and made plans to return to the Patriots.

Gould became Public Enemy No. 2 to Patriots media and fans. He was criticized for not giving Glenn the proper advice, when all along Gould was trying to get Glenn to return to camp.

Feeling his client got an unfair ruling on his appeal with the commissioner's office, Gould hired the distinguished law firm of Williams and Connolly in Washington, D.C.

"We feel Terry got railroaded," said Gould. "It had nothing to do with a positive reading, it had to do with a missed phone call. We have no rights under the collective-bargaining process. We're taking it to the courts. We found this to be an absolute lack of due process. We're going to show that this program does not act in the best interests of the player."

Gould said "someone made a phone call to his cell phone" in an attempt to set up an off-season substance test. According to Gould, Glenn was "out of town" at the time. Gould and NFLPA administrator Stacey Robinson concurred that Glenn made a series of attempts to contact his medical adviser to let him know he wasn't able to take the test because he wasn't home.

"Within 36 hours of that call, Terry took the test and it was negative," said Gould.

Both management and the players' union administer the league's drug program.

"In this case, they [the commissioner] were judge and the jury," said Gould.

Belichick, in an August 7 press conference in Smithfield, revealed private details about Glenn's drug violations.

"It's not a first-time occurrence, this type of situation," said Belichick. "It's the first time he was suspended. It's not the first time we've been notified that there was a problem. . . . I don't know how many times this has happened, but I'd say at least three, maybe more. And in all the other cases when they've reviewed it, nothing's happened. It's just gone away, and in this case, they upheld it."

Gould had spent the day in Warren, Ohio, attending the funeral of another client, former Minnesota Vikings offensive lineman Korey

Stringer, who had died of heat stroke in August. When he was told of Belichick's comments, Gould said, "I have no idea what he's talking about. I'm shocked he said that. His comments reflect how out of control the coach of the New England Patriots is."

*   *   *

Glenn amassed some $10,000 in fines during his second suspension. He had failed to get on an exercise machine to test his sore hamstring, feeling the hamstring hurt too badly. He was out for six weeks.

Glenn was legitimately hurt. In fact, even after Belichick had cleared him to play, Glenn said trainer Ron O'Neil never told Glenn he was cleared to play. Evidently, O'Neil and Belichick were at loggerheads over this issue. Some feel it cost O'Neil his job, as the long-time trainer was dismissed in March and reassigned.

During this time, on November 25, Glenn appeared on WBZ-TV's *Sports Final* program after the station's reporter, Steve Burton, had convinced him to come on to discuss the game that day. The interview, a coup for the station, did Glenn a lot of damage as Glenn insinuated he was faking the injury.

Burton had been trying to get an interview with Glenn since the summer. In fact, Burton flew to Glenn's home in Columbus, Ohio, the same day that Jimy Williams was getting fired from the Red Sox. When Burton got there and met up with Glenn, "he [Glenn] pulled the plug on the interview. Apparently, his lawyer told him not to say anything because the grievance hearing was coming up. Terry felt bad about it, but he told me that he would eventually sit with me," Burton recalled.

To ensure Glenn's arrival in time for live TV, Glenn met Burton at a McDonald's opposite the Fleet Center; Glenn followed him back to the station from there.

Burton then told Glenn, who kept his sunglasses on for the interview, he needed to ask him about his personal situation and Glenn agreed.

The most memorable lines were when Burton asked, "So do you want to play for them [the Patriots] again?"

Glenn said, "I did want to play for them. That's d-i-d, *did*, but I don't think I'll be here next season. I don't care if I'm still on this football team."

Bob Lobel, WBZ-TV's sports director, who was also interviewing Glenn that night, asked whether his refusal to play was over the money the team owed him.

"Maybe. I'm not getting paid and my hamstring hurts. You do the math," said Glenn, startling the interviewer as well as the viewers. That statement hung Glenn.

After sitting out the Carolina game, the regular-season finale, he was fined once more for unexcused absences to meetings. According to Glenn all of his absences were excused.

Glenn said it hurt not to be a part of the playoffs and the Super Bowl, but "I think it was best, especially the way things went, that I wasn't around. They didn't need me. They've proved that. I'm not upset about it. In some ways I wish I were there because it was the Super Bowl, and I remember what that was like in 1996. But I needed to take care of what I had to take care of. I needed to get my life back to some sense of a normal existence."

But the lawsuits kept coming. During Super Bowl week, Glenn's lawyers filed a suit in U.S. District Court in Manhattan suing the NFL for failure to recognize that Glenn suffered from chronic depression, which was a recognized disability through the Americans with Disabilities Act. Glenn received very little sympathy.

After the season had finally ended, Glenn was asked whether he was depressed. He said, "With all that's happened, sure I am. It's been a tough year. I feel like I never played football this year for the first time in my life. I felt like I was just going through one bad thing after another. I just want it to end."

National Football League Players' Association president Gene Upshaw and general counsel Richard Berthelsen were hoping to reach a settlement. They met with Kraft during Super Bowl week about pushing forward with a resolution to the situation.

Glenn wound up missing out on a once-in-a-lifetime opportunity to be a part of a Super Bowl team. He watched the Super Bowl from his home in Columbus.

"It hurt, sure it hurt," said Glenn. "I was in this organization since the last Super Bowl. I would have loved to play in that game. I felt good for the people in that organization. I felt good for Mr. Kraft."

Although he received a full share of Super Bowl winnings, Glenn was not expecting a Super Bowl championship ring. "If they offer me one, I'll certainly accept it and keep it in my archives. It would be nice to get one."

Does he think he deserves one?

"Probably not. They probably don't think I deserve one after all that's happened. I would understand that. If I didn't get one I wouldn't be calling the Foxboro switchboard every day asking where it is or nothing like that. Whatever they decide is fine."

Gould and the Packers were able to work out a new contract, while the Packers and Patriots worked out the trade compensation. Glenn agreed to waive his grievances, and Kraft wound up walking away without having to pay the remaining $8.5 million of Glenn's bonus, freeing almost $3 million of cap space for the Patriots.

When it was all over, Belichick phoned Glenn to wish him the best in his future endeavors. The coach said afterward, "It's too bad. I wished it could have worked out."

CHAPTER **12**

The Rocky Road

The Patriots playing the Broncos in Denver is like a bird flying north for the winter. It usually doesn't work out very well.

Former Broncos linebacker Bill Romanowski, much like Cox, has been known to set the tone for a team. Before the Patriots-Broncos game, scheduled for October 29, the former Boston College star fired the first salvo when he said of the Patriots' trick plays against Indianapolis, "I am sure we'll practice them, but the trick plays over the years to me have shown a sign of weakness. But bottom line, they're making them work. They are putting points on the board with them, so it's hard to say anything bad about them. I'm just saying, over the years, that's what I've thought."

"Romo" probably didn't have to say a thing.

The weekly news surrounded the usual topics. One: would Glenn shake off the cobwebs and play? I think we knew the answer to that. Two: dressed in his familiar No. 11 Patriots jersey, Bledsoe threw several passes in Wednesday's practice for the first time since suffering internal injuries. Bledsoe threw distances of about 20 yards. He didn't take part in any of the team drills, but he said, "It's just great to get out there and hold and throw a football again. There's a

115

lot of gray area on exactly how much I can do, but basically I can do some as long as it doesn't hurt."

Bledsoe had lost about 20 pounds after his injuries, and for a while he looked pale and gaunt. Now it looked as if color was returning to his face. He had gained about 10 pounds, and he was able to act as the team's third quarterback in the game.

The theme of the week was the clash of former Michigan quarterbacks—Brady and Brian Griese. Interestingly, they were going in different directions with their popularity. New England fans wanted to marry Brady, while Broncos fans were ready to file for divorce with Griese.

Griese, a Denver Wolverine and a walk-on at Michigan, had beaten out Brady for the starting job. Though their relationship was strained a bit at the time, they were good friends now.

"He's a very smart guy. He knows what he's doing. I've been happy for him that he's having success. I look for him to continue to have that success. I expect him to play a smart game, not make any mistakes, and give his team a chance to win," said Griese.

That was the Michigan way.

Brady said Griese was a "mentally tough" person because he had lost his mother when he was very young. His father was Hall of Famer Brian Griese of Miami Dolphins fame. There were pressures while the younger Griese was growing up to live up to his father's fame.

Brady said he learned mental toughness from Griese by competing and playing with him. He said his battle with Griese also changed his outlook on the entire dynamic of competition.

"I spent too much time on how Brian or Scott Dreisbach was playing and I needed to spend more time on how I was playing. It's all about how I play and how I perform. It's not about what the other guys are doing. And that really helped me down the road."

Griese said of Brady, "Tom's been playing smarter football than Drew. That's why they're winning."

Not only that, the Patriots were winning because four major things were occurring: (1) they were not turning the ball over; (2) they had reduced the stupid penalties that had killed them in earlier games; (3) their red zone efficiency was improving (the Patriots had scored on 8 of their 13 chances since Brady took over); and (4) they were absorbing Belichick's leadership and coaching.

"There's a feeling we have some good players and good coaching," said Law. "We've always had a good feeling. We had some games early that we should have won, but we did things in those games that made us lose. But there was a lot of negativity and we just shut that out. We knew we were going to begin to turn it around. We just can't say it, we have to do it every week now."

It was definitely a new challenge to the team. Belichick had challenged them to climb the mountain one step at a time. He stressed short-term focus. The first order of business was to win a game. Then it was rebounding against Miami. Then it was winning a game on the road, which they did against Indy at the RCA Dome. Now, it was beating the Broncos in the toughest place to win on the road. You had to beat the altitude and the incredible home record the Broncos have amassed over the years.

Belichick was telling the team, "Our goal is not to have a bad day. I mean, I know someone's gonna drop a ball or miss a coverage. But you should never have a bad day. But what we have to stop is having that bad play affect the following play, and then you have a bunch of crummy plays. You cannot do that. If that happens, you're gonna have problems."

The coach admitted, "We have to be close to our best every week. If we just try to slap it out there and hope for the best, it's not going to happen."

* * *

After Brady threw four fourth-quarter interceptions in a 31–20 loss to the Broncos, dropping the Patriots to below .500 at 3–4, accolades he had received were being toned back. Teammates were taking the bullet for Brady, but the young QB was candid about his performance. "I'm the guy who needs to make those plays," said Brady, who threw 4 of his last 11 passes to the other team. "No excuses. I've just got to get better, and I will."

Brady had thrown 162 passes at the start of his career without an interception, an NFL record.

The loss wasn't all young Tom's fault. For instance, the Patriots were leading the game 20–10 in the third quarter when the defense had a mile-high lapse in brain function.

Rod Smith, Denver's best receiver and one of the best in the game, was allowed to cross over the middle untouched, catch a Griese strike at the 40, and then race down the sideline for a 65-yard score. That cut the lead to 20–17 with 10:35 remaining in the third quarter.

"There was a miscommunication on the coverage, and that's inexcusable," said a rather disgusted Milloy. "For Smith to beat us like that, that's hard to swallow. We were doubling him and I was the safety helping out over the top. It was a quick crossing play, and the corner thought I was going to be somewhere else. It's our job as a defense to put Tom in a stress-free situation, and we didn't do it."

It was a huge momentum shift because that play got the Denver defense going. The Broncos sacked Brady twice in the next series. It was three-and-out. Griese took control at the 20, and he picked the Patriots defense apart down the field. Matt Stevens, who was seeing less time with the emergence of Jones, made a huge blunder when he overpursued tight end Desmond Clark, who caught a pass and went down, but got back up and ran 35 yards.

"The whistle didn't blow. It was an alert play by them and not so alert by us," lamented Belichick, who later put Stevens on the expansion list; Stevens was taken by the Houston Texans.

Griese finally capped the long drive with a six-yard touchdown toss to tight end Dwayne Carswell with 3:35 remaining in the third quarter. The Broncos were up 24–20.

Suddenly Brady had to shift from protecting the lead and running down the clock to regaining the lead and the momentum. The kid did a good job of it for a while. Brady started the Patriots' next drive from the 22 and took them all the way down to the Broncos' 13. Unfortunately, Brady, under pressure on third-and-12, threw off-balance into the back of the end zone toward Patten, who was moving from left to right. But Denard Walker stepped in front of Patten and picked it off.

Then, Brady, trying to throw the ball about 30 yards upfield to Patten on a third-and-3, saw Deltha O'Neal make a tremendous over-the-shoulder diving interception.

But the worst was Brady throwing a ball into no-man's-land where Walker picked it off and ran 39 yards for a touchdown and the Broncos' final score.

"I take most of the blame for the loss," said Troy Brown, who was the intended receiver on the final interception. "I was out there reading the defense and I didn't get on the same page. He threw it to the outside and I went inside. My fault."

The fourth Denver pickoff was a desperation late-game toss that really didn't matter much except that it showed up on the stat sheet.

Brady had a 137.2 quarterback rating in the first half after completing 13 of 16 for 113 yards, two touchdowns, and no interceptions. Heck, through three quarters he was 21 for 24 for 163 yards. But that plummeted like the New England weather, and Brady ended the day with a 57.1 rating.

Brady was superb in the first half. He led the team downfield for an Adam Vinatieri field goal on the first drive of the game. Then, on the second series, following a tough defensive stand by the Patriots, Brady continued to take the Broncos' crowd out of the game, making a tough throw under pressure to Brown for 18 yards. That was compounded when a flagrant 15-yard face mask was tacked on.

At the Denver 30, Brady dropped back, waited for Patten to break into the clear past O'Neal, and laid a bullet into Patten's chest making it 10–0.

When the Denver offense stepped back onto the field, Griese was hearing boos, especially after McGinest sacked him to a two-yard loss.

Griese needed to do something, so he found Rod Smith open down the right sideline for a 47-yard gain to the Patriots' 35. Griese eventually hit Clark with a 20-yard touchdown pass, making it a 10–7 game.

The Patriots were quickly losing momentum.

The double-pass that had worked so well against Indianapolis failed miserably this time. Why it was tried in back-to-back games was another mystery. This time Patten's pass to Charles Johnson was short and was intercepted at the 2-yard line by safety Eric Brown. The Broncos turned that turnover into a 50-yard field goal by Jason Elam to tie the score.

But the Patriots took the lead before the half. First Bruschi intercepted Griese in an interesting sequence. Bruschi then fumbled the ball and it appeared as though Griese had recovered it. But Cox wrestled it away from him at the Broncos' 32. A frustrated Griese kicked Cox and drew an unsportsmanlike penalty of 15 more yards. Two plays later, Brady found Brown alone in the back of the end zone on a four-yard pass for the go-ahead score.

At this point, Brady was really excited. Denver linebacker Al Wilson felt he was too excited, too talkative for a young kid, and decided to lay a shoulder into his chest.

Said Wilson, "I told him, 'You'd better play 60 minutes, boy, or it can get ugly.' Only I told him in more vulgar language. And it did get ugly. It got ugly for us, and it got ugly for Brady."

After Belichick watched the tape of the game on Monday he came away saying, "I don't think he had a tough fourth quarter. I think he had one throw that was not a good throw and I think two of the interceptions really weren't his fault."

Unfortunately for the Patriots, not only did they lose the game, they also lost Cox. On a cheap play, offensive lineman Stephen Neal cut blocked Cox beyond the area between the tackles, where cut blocks are not allowed. The officials didn't even call a penalty; either they didn't see it or they didn't believe it.

Cox's leg was broken in two places, an eerily similar injury to the one that cut his season short with the Jets the year before.

"To be honest, I don't care if it takes the rest of my career, if I ever play that guy he's gonna have a blown-out knee and I don't care who knows it because he just does that sort of [bleep] all the time. He cuts me like that and then he has the [bleeping] audacity to ask me if I'm all right. No, I'm not [bleeping] alright!" Cox railed.

Cox thought the play was part of a bigger problem. He accused the Broncos of teaching cheap shots. Denver linemen had been fined on numerous occasions for cheap cut blocks. But Cox was skeptical they would fine Neal because "This league is known for going out of its way to protect the quarterback, but they couldn't care less about the rest of us." The NFL later fined Neal $15,000 after the league reviewed the play.

Cox eventually settled down and surprised everyone early the following week when he said he was going to send Neal a letter of apology for his comments.

"After talking to my lady and my friends, I realized that because something unfortunate happens to me, or because something happens that I think is wrong, I don't wish anybody injury as a result of something that happened to me. I need to apologize because in my frustration I told him I was going to blow out his knee. I don't want to see anybody injured in that capacity," Cox said.

Considered one of NFL's bad boys, Cox was trying to be the Good Bryan.

Cox's being out of the game was a big loss for the Patriots. Cox had played well, he was physical, and he was a true leader on the field. He said of his role from here on out, "I can be an extra set of eyes. I'll be talking to the younger guys, guys like Mike Vrabel, and I'll be talking and giving my opinion if asked."

* * *

Midseason had arrived. The Patriots dug out of an 0–2 and 1–3 hole, climbed back to .500, only to slip back versus Denver. It was crunch time—either make something of the season or fall back.

Mistakes and lapses in concentration were still abundant. The Patriots knew what they were doing wrong, but as Milloy so aptly said, "If we recognize what we're doing wrong but don't change it, what good is that?"

It was quite a moment for Brady, too. The biggest proof of a person's mettle is how he or she responds to adversity, a fact that Bill Parcells pointed out that week on his radio show on WWZN-1510 in Boston. He said if a player learns from his mistakes and turns his problems into pluses, then he's a player.

Well, Brady proved he was a player.

In the Georgia Dome in Atlanta on November 4, Brady handled the first game of the rest of his life with class, dignity, and high performance. He completed 21 of 31 passes for 250 yards, three touchdown passes, and *no* interceptions. He threw the ball to eight different receivers.

The Patriots won the game, 24–10.

Brady's rebound didn't surprise his teammates.

Patten said, "We expected this. We knew last week was one of those games. Every great quarterback has them. Tom has the potential to be a great quarterback in this league, so it's no shock to any of us."

Brady completed four of his first nine passes. He missed a couple of chances down the field, but in the second quarter he was machinelike, completing 15 of 17.

"It would take a while to get my confidence down," said Brady. "It would take a few bad games in a row. There have been hard times I've had before the Denver game. You learn to deal with them and just move forward."

The Patriots got 117 yards from Antowain Smith, whose timely running helped the Patriots control the clock. It was the first 100-yard rushing game by a Patriot since Terry Allen ran for 126 yards against the Dolphins on December 26, 1999. "We needed to get the running game going to take the pressure off Brady," said Smith. "Once we got it established we were able to execute some play-action passes."

Eight different defenders sacked a combination of Chris Chandler and No. 1 pick Michael Vick nine times. McGinest, who played his best game yet, was the only player with two sacks.

McGinest, who had off-season surgery in June to fix some disks in his back, said, "You've got to understand that if you've had major surgery on your back you're not going to bounce right back. I feel good now. I just want to buckle it up and go."

Pleasant knocked Chandler out of the game with an unpleasant shot to the ribs right before the end of the third quarter. As much as Weis had been lauded for his perfect game plans, defensive coordinator Romeo Crennel, who was often overshadowed by the presence of Belichick, came up with a pretty solid game plan. It called for going after Chandler hard.

"If you say you're going to blitz, you'd better get there," said defensive end Bobby Hamilton.

Weis could pat himself on the back as well. Going into the week, he knew the Falcons would try to take away Brown and Patten, so he incorporated his running backs into the passing game. Smith, Faulk, and Edwards accounted for 10 catches and two touchdowns.

But the Patriots didn't start well. Smith fumbled on the Falcons' 14-yard line and the Falcons turned that error into seven points. Falcons running back Maurice Smith popped a 58-yard run when Jones came in on a blitz, leaving Jones' side wide open. Chandler then hit former Patriots receiver Shawn Jefferson for a 19-yard touchdown pass.

But the Patriots really seemed to believe in their game plan. There was no panic. Answering the Atlanta challenge, Brady strung together a 16-play, 75-yard drive, short-to-medium passes the whole way.

On third down from the 4-yard line, the Patriots used a five-receiver, empty backfield as Brady lofted a fade to the left corner to Faulk, covered by linebacker Keith Brooking, to tie the score.

The 36-year-old Chandler had been very efficient and in fact had kept Vick on the bench. But the Patriots never allowed him to get into rhythm. In the second quarter, Chandler tried throwing over the middle to Jefferson, but Otis Smith stepped in and returned the interception 17 yards to the 26.

Four penalties on the drive kept pushing the Patriots back to the point where they had to settle for Vinatieri's 48-yard field goal giving them a 10–7 lead.

Making his homecoming special, Seymour, the former Georgia star, showed he was over early season hamstring woes, overpowering his man and sacking Chandler for a six-yard loss late in the second quarter, forcing the Falcons to punt.

With 2:56 remaining and starting the drive at the 11, Brady marched the Patriots 89 yards on 10 plays. Brady connected with Brown on a 25-yard pass to the Patriots' 48. Later, Brady hit a wide-open Edwards, who stumbled but kept his feet moving, on a 15-yard touchdown pass.

The Patriots led 17–7 at halftime.

To this point, third quarters had been a nightmare for the Patriots; they had been outscored 69–16. But this time, the defense was tough.

The Patriots acted out their version of the "Immaculate Reception" when, with 44 seconds remaining in the third quarter, Brady threw toward Patten at the Patriots' 15. The ball never got to Patten, tipping off Falcons cornerback Ashley Ambrose's right knee and bouncing to Brown instead. Brown ran it 44 yards in the clear to the end zone to seal the victory.

"Franco Harris," said Brown mentioning the name of the player who came up with the original Immaculate Reception. "When I was running, I was thinking about him."

With the statuesque Chandler out, the more elusive Vick broke loose for a 35-yard scamper at one point, but the Patriots eventually got the hang of it. Vick completed only two of nine passes and was sacked three times.

He could run, but he could not hide.

The Patriots, .500 at midseason, flew home that night pretty happy.

With the AFC East bunched up with teams at or around .500, they knew they controlled their destiny.

* * *

After Patriots executives landed in Boston, they met with Glenn and Gould to discuss a game plan for how Glenn was to be handled the rest of the season. The next day Glenn admitted he suffered from chronic depression and his attorneys filed a complaint with the Equal Employment Opportunity Commission against the National Football League, saying depression was the reason the receiver was unable to take his mandated drug test. The EEOC granted a "right to sue" document. It was the story that wouldn't go away.

CHAPTER 13

Sign and Return, Please

The Patriots were 4–4, even Steven, 0–0; the slate was clean. Everything was ahead of them. Moving forward, however, required some "self-evaluation," as coach Belichick often did.

Usually .500 teams get a C. Logical, right? But this was a team improving by the week. If it was an F to start, it moved quickly to D, then to a C, and it was probably a little better than that. But how did the individual players score?

> **Quarterback: B**. Brady was 4–2 as a starter with a quarterback rating of 90. The sample size with which to properly evaluate him was growing, and he kept improving. He had the slipup in Denver, but he really bounced back strong against the Falcons. To this point, the kid had tackled all of the big challenges, and for the most part he had answered them. In the second half he would have to answer the following questions: Would he be able to avoid a slump after teams began to game plan against him? Would he hit a wall?

Running back: B minus. Showing signs of getting stronger, Smith had already produced a 100-yard-plus game, and more important, he was gaining big yards, chewing up the clock, and giving the Patriots a threat of a running game, which they hadn't had since Robert Edwards' rookie season in 1998. Averaging 3.8 yards per carry as a team, the Patriots had an outside chance of gaining four yards per carry for the first time since 1985. Their offensive attack was still not completely balanced, however. They were 22nd in the league in rushing, averaging 104.5 yards and 27.6 running plays per game. But they were on the right track.

Wide receiver: B. For the second consecutive season the Patriots had basically a two-man receiving core. Such lack of depth was a killer for Bledsoe in 2000, but not so for Brady through his six games. In 2000 Brown and Glenn combined for 78 catches, 39 apiece at midseason. In 2001 Brown and Patten had caught 82 passes, 53 of them to Brown, who was having an outstanding season. The big difference was touch-downs . . . points . . . pay dirt. The receivers had seven TDs at the break, compared to five in 2000. An effective third receiver would have eased the pressure of keeping two receivers healthy for an entire season. Somehow they didn't need that.

Tight end: D. The Patriots had nine catches in eight games at this position. Bledsoe had nicknamed Wiggins "7-Eleven: Always Open" in 2000, but so far there had been a "closed" sign hanging on the backs of Wiggins and Rutledge. Wiggins was the receiver, Rutledge the blocker. But neither was getting his hand close to a football. The Patriots tried to upgrade the position in the draft by taking Notre Dame's Jabari Holloway and South Carolina State's Arther Love. However, both were injured. Holloway was placed on injured reserve, ending his season in training camp. Love was placed on the physically unable to perform list, then was activated, though he never saw action on the active roster.

Offensive line: B. Most improved? Hands down. They got off to a slow start in training camp with virtually all five starters coming down with injuries. They jelled in a hurry. Compton and Andruzzi had provided leadership and toughness. They had developed a streetfighter mentality. Woody continued to emerge as one of the best centers in the league, although he was still unable to shotgun snap. Robinson-Randall was the quiet man in the group, but the 23-year-old second-year player wasn't getting beat too often. Rookie Light was brash, tough, and cocky and added quickness and athleticism to this very important position.

Defensive line: B. Another emerging unit. McGinest had been in and out while healing his back, but Pleasant and Hamilton, who had 4.5 sacks to his credit after eight games, were certainly on top of their games. Pleasant was a favorite among players and coaches on the team. He was one of the hardest-working players and set a tremendous example for the younger players. He effectively assumed the role of Henry Thomas, another veteran leader, who had acted as a second coach on the football field in 2000.

Seymour was emerging as a force in the middle.

"We have a lot of confidence as a unit now," said Hamilton. "The more we play together and experience game conditions, the better we get."

The Patriots were beginning to make the switch to a 4-3 defense where Seymour was able to play a more natural position head-up on a guard rather than center. Mitchell was rotating quite a bit but definitely had resurrected his career. When McGinest didn't play, the Patriots didn't have that traditional pass rusher type, but they were pressuring the quarterback.

Linebackers: B. Phifer was having a career season. "He's my MVP," declared Buckley. Phifer had always been a good cover linebacker, but while replacing McGinest at the rush position during McGinest's recovery, Phifer showed he could pressure and run down the passer as well. And he could stop the run.

Bruschi, who had played a mind-boggling 1,200 plays in 2000, was playing virtually every down after Cox suffered his broken leg against Denver.

Vrabel, who had started his first eight games in the league after spending three seasons with Pittsburgh as a sub, was everything the Patriots had hoped for in coverage, in blitzing, and against the run. Ted Johnson's time was diminishing. As the Patriots went more to a 4-3, Bruschi was used in the middle, replacing Johnson. They were active as a unit, making plays.

Defensive backs: B. Belichick liked what he saw from this unit. Otis Smith was aging but effective. Law was slowly returning to the player he had been in the late nineties: tough and hard to beat.

Milloy was the same from the first game through the 19th: consistent and tough as nails. The strong safety had assumed new responsibilities in coverage and in the running game, and he was handling them well.

Jones was definitely a force in the making. For the first two years of his career he was wasted as a cornerback, when his true niche was beating the snot out of the opponent. He created an intimidation factor, but he needed to tackle better and wrap up the opponent, rather than just lay a shoulder or a helmet into him.

Special teams: C. This was the unit that struggled at times in the first half of the season but came on to be a true force in the second half. The problems with punter Johnson were well documented, and then Walter took a couple of games to get used to his surroundings before he began to excel. The Patriots were allowing the second-highest return average (26.1 yards), and part of the problem was Vinatieri's hang time, but his field goals were not a problem, converting 13 out of 14 by midseason.

The Patriots never really got their kick return situation straightened out, starting with Faulk, before he became ineffective. Jones, Izzo, and Je'Rod Cherry were making plays on cover teams, while Troy Brown hadn't yet brought one to the house on punt returns, but the best was yet to come.

* * *

A wave of optimism floated through the locker room, a team suddenly believing there was a legitimate shot at making the playoffs.

"Why not?" said Woody. "We're getting better week after week. If we can avoid mistakes and play our game there's no reason we can't be a playoff team. We're 4–4, and that's like 0–0. What we do the rest of the way, we can control that."

The optimism was also aroused because the Patriots were starting the second half playing the 1–6 Buffalo Bills. Certainly Belichick was pumping up the opponent, as he often did. He always told his players to respect the opponent and never take anyone lightly. He meant that and got that message across very well.

Belichick kept saying the difference between being 1–6 and 4–3 was "a couple of plays here and there." When he said it, it always sounded like gibberish, and then you'd see what he meant.

"You just have to look and see the films of their games and you'll see all you need to see from Buffalo," said Belichick.

After taking two out of three on the road, the Patriots were starting a three-game home stand. As the weather began deteriorating, Foxboro Stadium gave them a home-field advantage.

"This is our house," said Milloy. "We have a chance to do something positive here. We're 0–0 as far as we're concerned. If we put together a good second half, we'll be in the playoffs. It's right in front of us, and now we have to take it."

During the week the Patriots submitted to the league office an 18-player injury list that included starting offensive tackles, the entire starting defensive line, and the team's top three receivers. Belichick was concerned. "We have a lot of bumps and bruises. We have a lot of guys who are getting over things," he said.

One theory was that Belichick wanted to give the impression the Patriots were the ailing puppy to create some type of a letdown by the Bills.

Unable to wait for Glenn to get back on the practice field, the team signed former XFL receiver Fred Coleman to a contract for the remainder of the season. Coleman had played for the Chicago Enforcers. Before that he had played at the University of Washington, where he caught 97 passes (some of them from Patriots backup Damon Huard) for 1,588 yards.

Coleman became one of those complementary players who made a couple of impossible plays to help the Impossible Team.

CHAPTER 14

Mr. Smith Goes to Pay Dirt

That Antowain Smith signed a five-year deal worth more than $20 million with a $3 million two-tiered signing bonus on March 1, 2002, was not surprising. He had effectively resurrected a fledgling career after spending two years as a backup player with the Buffalo Bills, buried on the depth chart by offensive coordinator Joe Pendry, who had since left the team.

Smith was a No. 1 draft pick out of the University of Houston in 1998 and rushed for 1,124 yards as a 25-year-old rookie with the Bills.

Smith started his NFL career late because he made a commitment to care for his ailing grandparents, Clara and John Smith, who raised him in Millbrook, Alabama. He turned down a chance to play ball at Auburn University to work at Gurney Manufacturing in Prattville, Alabama, from 1990 to 1993, where he dyed cloth for $4.60 an hour.

After the Bills released him, there were reports that new general manager Tom Donahoe said Smith was unwilling to take part in the strength and conditioning program. That's why Donahoe let him go.

The Patriots had certainly done their homework on Smith; they knew of his background and his commitment to his grandparents. They knew Smith was a hard worker and precisely the tough, downfield runner they were looking for.

"I knew the division, the teams, and I had performed against the Patriots for four years," said Smith. "They didn't have a lead running back and I knew I'd get a legitimate chance to be the starter again. I took it, and I've never regretted it. We won the Super Bowl."

It was tough for Smith not to feel something extra on November 11 when the Patriots played the Buffalo Bills in the first of their two-game series. There was already great anticipation in the air with the second half of the season starting, and the Patriots were on the upswing thanks to the inspiring play of Smith and some of the other free-agent veterans acquired in the off-season.

"He was very excited that day," recalled Brady. "You could tell when he walked in that morning that he really wanted to make an impression. He came out and ran hard—he always runs hard—even there at the end, he was real excited to break that one off."

The one he "broke off" was a 42-yard run for a touchdown, which sealed a 21–11 win over the Bills. Smith ran 20 times for 100 yards, his second consecutive 100-yard game and a feat he had never performed in his career.

Funny thing is he wasn't having the greatest day until then, basically grinding out three yards per carry. But Smith always seemed to come up with the big play at the most opportune time.

It wasn't an easy 42-yard run either.

Smith took Brady's handoff, which was designed to be a simple dive up the middle. The Bills were ready for it, piling up on him at the line of scrimmage, but Smith somehow Houdinied his way out of it, breaking a tackle by Travares Tillman, then cutting back. He got into the clear and was off to the races.

"Some of the players were like, 'Dawg, how did you get out of that?'" Smith said. "To break the one to put us over the top and seal it, that felt great."

Smith, who now had 574 yards in nine games, claimed no personal vendetta against the Bills, saying, "That's a whole new coaching staff. There's nobody on that staff that was there when they drafted me or when I played there for four years. I have nothing against them. Actually, I have nothing against the other coaching staff. I know the confidence I have in myself that I can still play and help a team win. And I'm just making the most of my opportunity here."

* * *

We heard the word *luck* after this game.

Troy Brown said, "We were lucky to win the game. That's a pretty good football team."

The word of the day should have been *ugly*. That best described it. But it was a win nonetheless, and the Patriots needed those a lot more than they needed losses.

The Patriots were over .500, 5–4, and the Bills were 1–7.

Buffalo's defense found a way to contain Brady, taking away the dink-and-dunk passing game. "You'd like to play great every week," said Brady, "but that's not the case in this league, as I'm finding out."

Brady was sacked seven times, threw one interception, and fumbled twice. If the Bills' offense could have slightly improved their 2-for-12 conversion ratio on third down, the outcome might have been different.

The Patriots had taken a 7–0 lead with 3:09 remaining in the first quarter when Brady tossed a six-yard TD pass to Faulk. The drive started at the Bills' 35 thanks to a 29-yard punt return by Troy Brown as Brian Moorman's boot got caught in a swirling wind, making it low and very returnable. Brown saw a hole on the left side and ran as hard as he could through it before being taken down.

The Bills responded with a Jake Arians 24-yard field goal after the Bills connected on their longest pass play of the game, a 36-yard catch by tight end Jay Riemersma, who was wide open and ran it down to the Patriots' 9-yard line.

The Patriots squandered a big chance to score in the second quarter when Faulk coughed up the ball at the Bills' 15-yard line after Brady had run a nice drive from the Patriots' 32. But Faulk's goat horns were soon removed when Otis Smith picked off Johnson, which led to the first of two missed field goals by Vinatieri, who was battling an impossible wind.

With 7:23 remaining in the third quarter, the Patriots finally added some excitement to what had been a boring afternoon. Patten drew a 25-yard penalty on Antoine Winfield, who had groped him in the end zone. From there, Smith dove from the 1-yard line to give the Patriots a 14–3 lead.

In the fourth quarter, the Patriots held only a three-point lead, 14–11. The Bills pulled close when linebacker Kendrick Office forced a Brady fumble as the quarterback was backtracking to get away from the pressure, and Jay Foreman at the Patriots' 17 recovered the ball.

Buffalo quarterback Alex Van Pelt replaced Rob Johnson earlier in the quarter when Buckley injured him on a corner blitz. Two plays later, Van Pelt connected with Peerless Price in the end zone. Van Pelt then executed the two-point conversion with a pass to Eric Moulds over Law, making it a three-point game.

That's why Smith's run, with just 1:52 remaining, was huge.

Given what was ahead—the St. Louis Rams—the Patriots felt a little uneasy about the way they won the game.

"We're going to have to be at our best. We can't afford to make mistakes or turn the ball over. We've got to be on our game," said Woody.

Brown was more succinct: "If we play like we did today next Sunday, we won't win the game. You're talking about the team that a lot of people think is the best in football right now."

Brady had this to say: "We know if we want to be the best, we have to beat the best. The Rams have been great for a couple of years now. It's been exciting for us. We are back at home in front of our own fans and it is going to be a night game, and everyone is going to be watching. So we're going to put our best effort out there."

Vinatieri made what proved to be the most poignant observation: "The Ravens were 5–4 at this point last year. And they were the Super Bowl champions."

*   *   *

As good as Smith felt about the Buffalo game, he felt a pain in his gut after the Rams beat the Patriots, 24–17, at Foxboro Stadium on November 18.

A 14-point swing prior to the end of the first half was triggered by Smith's fumble at the Rams' 4-yard line caused by a London Fletcher hit. Rams cornerback Aeneas Williams dove for the loose ball and held it tight as the Patriots players tried to retake it. The Patriots argued Smith's knee was down prior to the ball popping loose and they challenged the play; but the call on the field was upheld by referee Bill Leavy, who felt the replay was inconclusive.

"I have to blame myself," said Smith. "It's not all right in that situation. I'm a veteran. I've got to have better ball security in that situation. I felt I was down. I felt my knee was down or my progress had been stopped. I felt like we were going to score a touchdown. I have to put it behind real fast. We had an opportunity to shock the world—that turnover killed us."

Don't worry, Antowain, that opportunity would come again.

If the Patriots had scored, they would have led 17–7. Instead they trailed, 14–10, after the Rams marched 97 yards after the fumble.

"We left a lot on the field," said Otis Smith. "We had to spread our defense to match what they had to offer. We let them score, which we shouldn't do. We should never let them march 97 yards like that. Never."

Just before Smith's fumble, Belichick made one of many gutsy calls during the season. It was fourth-and-2 from the Rams' 44 when he decided to go for it. Understand, if they don't make this, the best offense in football gets the ball at their own 44. That's great field position. The Patriots not only got the necessary 2 yards but 15 extra—17 altogether—when Brady found Brown open on the right flat.

That should have been a huge momentum-builder, but Smith's fumble erased it and then some.

Kurt Warner needed only nine plays, completing seven passes in 1:41 to lead the Rams down the field, capping off the drive with a nine-yard pass to Marshall Faulk.

"That was vintage Kurt," said Rams head coach Mike Martz.

The Patriots didn't start the game very crisply, either.

The crowd at Foxboro was pretty loud and excited. This was the Patriots' only night game of the regular season, facing the best team in football. On the first series, which started at their own 9-yard line, the Patriots silenced their fans—not a good thing. Brady went back to throw and spotted Kevin Faulk crossing over the middle. Faulk let the ball bounce off his fingertips into the hands of Dexter McLeon at the 18.

Warner, who was nursing a sore thumb, didn't show any ill effects as he brought the Rams down the field with precision, finally spotting Torry Holt in stride on a post pattern for 16 yards with 9:38 remaining in the first quarter.

Belichick and Crennel kept emphasizing to the defense that they had to stop the Rams in the middle of the field. That's where they were the most dangerous. The message wasn't heard enough on that night.

The Patriots answered the Rams' first-quarter score when Buckley took advantage of veteran receiver Ricky Proehl's running the wrong route, as Buckley intercepted Warner at the 48 and took it 52 yards for the score.

Ironically, Buckley, who had returned five interceptions for touchdowns in his career, had last done it against Warner in 2000 when he was a member of the Denver Broncos.

"He [Warner] chewed my ass," said Proehl of his error.

The mistakes kept on coming.

On the Rams' next possession, the Patriots tried flooding the backfield with six and sometimes seven defensive backs to fill the zones where the speedy receivers were traveling.

"I thought that was illegal," quipped Martz on the Patriots using seven DBs at one time.

On that play Warner tried to drill one into Marshall Faulk when Bruschi intercepted at the Rams' 40.

After Brown caught a 23-yard pass on a ball thrown behind him, the Patriots settled for a 33-yard field goal by Vinatieri with 14:04 remaining in the half, now up 10–7. Usually sure-footed Jeff Wilkins missed a field goal from 42 yards, but then the sequence of events involving Smith allowed the Rams to score before the end of the half.

The Rams, up 17–10 in the fourth quarter, scored again on an 11-yard pass from Warner to fullback James Hodgkins to make it 24–10 with 10:32 remaining.

The Patriots were up for the fight. Brady calmly drove his team 65 yards in 2:46, connecting on all five pass attempts, including a 27-yard strike to Patten to the Rams' 21. Two plays later, Brady spotted Patten alone in the corner of the end zone to pull the Patriots to within one score with 7:46 remaining.

Now, if only the Patriots could stop the Rams quickly and get the ball back to mount the tying drive.

Never happened.

The Rams offense held the ball for the remaining 7:46. Warner took three knees deep in Patriots territory, and the game ended. The Rams had 482 yards of total offense to the Patriots' 230. They had 396 passing yards to the Patriots' 179.

If not a win, the Patriots gained some much-needed respect after this game. Martz boldly predicted a day later that the Patriots would be representing the AFC in the Super Bowl.

Was he serious?

Apparently so.

Throughout the week the game had been billed as Dr. Offense (Martz) versus Dr. Defense (Belichick). Belichick, asked about the Rams offense, which was averaging 31.9 points and 417.3 yards per game, said, "As long as I've been in the National Football League [26 years], this is the most explosive offense I've ever seen. Every play is a potential touchdown from any point on the field. They just keep coming. The skill players are tremendous, the quarterback is tremendous. The only way to stop their passing game is to let the air out of the ball, but that doesn't help either because they'll run for 300 yards."

* * *

Brady, now 5–3 as the starter, completed an efficient 19 for 27 for 185 yards, but he threw one touchdown and was intercepted twice.

When asked about his performance he said, "Ask Bill Belichick about that."

We did.

"We had our chances. We had some dropped balls and missed throws," said Belichick.

Brady's performance level was of utmost importance because, for the first week since he was nearly killed, Bledsoe was cleared to play by a staff of doctors at Massachusetts General Hospital. Bledsoe was on the sideline as the backup quarterback. He had started 122 games and had missed 6 due to injury since he was drafted No. 1 out of Washington in 1993. But this was the first time he was physically fit and standing on the sideline.

Of course, for this game it wasn't a real issue. Bledsoe hadn't played in seven weeks. Belichick was more than aware that the talk shows and the fans were discussing whether Bledsoe should start over Brady. But for Belichick, it was never an issue.

"We're going to poll the coaches, fans, fourth-graders, the barbers," kidded Belichick. "I understand everyone's talking about it.

There's a lot of interest in this team and there's nobody gladder than I am about it. In terms of making decisions, what the polls, the speculation, and controversy say, that's outside."

That week a Boston.com poll asked who should start at quarterback, and 78 percent of the respondents voted for Brady. Belichick's decision was far more unanimous than that.

Bledsoe had stirred the pot a bit during the week when he said, "I'm going to do everything in my power to get ready to play this football game."

Belichick said, "That's what every player should do. That's what this game is all about. That's what a competitor should do. . . . Drew has not practiced with the offensive football team for seven weeks. He has not taken one snap in seven weeks. How's he gonna look when he starts doing that? I don't know. I haven't seen it."

Even Brady praised Bledsoe for his comments.

"That's the competitiveness," said Brady. "You expect him to say that. Who doesn't want that? Go to the backup running back and he'll say the same thing. If you don't want that, you're in the wrong line of work."

It was still an uneasy time for the Patriots. They were 5–5 and preparing to play the tough Saints, and the Bledsoe story was on the brink of being a distraction.

CHAPTER 15

Bledsoe's Legacy

Trust means everything—in life and in sports. Was there a breach of trust between Bledsoe and Belichick, or did the coach simply reserve the right to change his mind for the good of the team when he told Bledsoe he'd be competing for the job one week and giving the job permanently to Brady the next?

While it may have been semantics to some, it was a thorny issue to Bledsoe.

Bledsoe's version of the story, according to those who would know, is that Belichick looked him in the eye upon his return the week of the St. Louis game and told him he would have a fair shot at winning the job back from Brady.

The day after a 24–17 loss to the Rams, Belichick told the team—after telling Bledsoe and Brady—that he was sticking with Brady, barring "something unforeseen."

That "unforeseen" was an ankle injury, which Brady incurred during the AFC championship game against Pittsburgh, resulting in Bledsoe leading the Patriots to a win and a Super Bowl berth.

Players I spoke to off the record the day of the announcement characterized Bledsoe as "angry" and said that Bledsoe and Belichick had engaged in a "very heated" conversation. Bryan Morry in *Patriots Football Weekly* rebuffed this in a report. But I still believe that choice words were exchanged.

Twice, Bledsoe had conversations with Kraft, with whom he had forged a strong bond, almost father-son–like. Kraft listened to Bledsoe, but he stayed out of it.

On November 20, Bledsoe came as close as he's ever been to blasting away. In the past he had bit his lip and always said the right thing. He did that to some degree on this day as well, but his curt answers to questions posed by *Patriots Football Weekly's* Paul Perillo and Associated Press reporter Jimmy Golen, spoke volumes.

Belichick and Bledsoe, asked about Bledsoe's emotions after learning the news of his demotion, gave similar responses: "You'll have to ask Drew," said Belichick.

Emotions?

"Next question," said Bledsoe.

Asked if it had been his understanding that he would compete with Brady, Bledsoe said, "That's what I was told."

If I may digress for a moment, why football players and coaches simply don't say what they really feel has always escaped me. There's always been this self-importance associated with head coach or star player, as if they're President Bush or Vice President Dick Cheney and discussing national security. Heck, in my dealings with President Bush when he was owner of the Texas Rangers, he understood more than anyone that he was overseeing a sports team, not the country.

Professional sports are supposed to be fun.

As frank as he could be, Belichick said he changed his mind because he didn't feel he could devote time to preparing both quarterbacks so late in the season. It was all about practice reps. Belichick believed the guy starting should get as many as possible.

Belichick said it wasn't about "Drew losing his job or being beaten out. It's strictly about the team. Nobody has done more for this organization than Drew Bledsoe. He's a consummate professional. It's tough anytime you have to tell anybody on the team

Bledsoe's Legacy

something they don't want to hear. Someone you have the utmost respect for."

Even in the spring after the Super Bowl when Belichick was asked again about the Bledsoe incident, all he would say was, "Nothing's changed. I wasn't holding back anything then. Whatever I said then is the way I feel about it now."

Asked if there were hard feelings between he and Bledsoe a month after the Super Bowl victory, Belichick said, "Not from my end."

Bledsoe made an interesting comment about possibly regaining his job the week he was cleared to play.

He said, "I've said on a number of occasions that nothing is promised to anybody in this game. From the time I was very young in this game, I felt that I had to go out and prove it on a daily basis. Since I've been in this league, since I was a rookie, I've been the starter. And I anticipate being the starter again. That being said, I've got to prove it again. I've got to establish that I'm the best guy for the job and that I'm the best guy who gives us a chance to win football games. At no time has, for whatever reason, it been promised to me that I'm going to be the starter regardless of what happens. Anybody that thinks otherwise is sorely mistaken."

Bledsoe was never able to establish that he was "the guy."

After Belichick named his quarterback for the New Orleans game, Bledsoe, obviously upset, said his peace, then reverted to what he's been since he got here—classy—putting the team ahead of his individual issues.

"My reaction is to simply do the same things I've done for nine years, since I was drafted by this team. And that is to do whatever it takes to help this team win. In this case, that means helping Tom [Brady] on the field and during the week," Bledsoe said.

Frustrated?

"Next question," said Bledsoe.

Bledsoe always had his staunch supporters, and he still does, but Brady had taken the region by storm. It was the minority who felt Bledsoe should get his job back, but if you believe the old sports

145

adage that you can't lose your job to injury, then you believed Bledsoe should be starting against the New Orleans Saints in week 11 of the NFL season with the team 5–5.

Many of those close to Bledsoe believed he got a raw deal.

Patriots fans in general, especially in retrospect, thought Belichick did the right thing.

You couldn't help but muster some sympathy for Bledsoe.

I have often commented that Bledsoe is the classiest athlete I've come across in 21 years of professional sportswriting. Some would say *boring*, but he is a good employee and a good teammate. Nobody would ever deny that.

It's funny how things worked out. Back on September 23 when Lewis delivered the blow, it seemed like a devastating situation for the Patriots. Instead, Brady came out of the blue, the rest of the team solidified, and you know the rest of the story.

Another bothersome aspect of the Bledsoe story was the lack of information on his condition. Again, the nation learned more about President Bush choking on a pretzel and all of the details associated with that than about Bledsoe's internal injuries. Bledsoe's father, Mac, a passionate man who does a tremendous job with the Drew Bledsoe Foundation's Parenting with Dignity program, said, "Why don't you guys write about how serious Drew's injury was?" Well, at the time, we didn't know. The only person speaking on the topic was Dr. Belichick.

It wasn't until November 13 that doctors at Massachusetts General Hospital finally explained it. This was after weeks of news outlets in the city reporting their own version of the story. The *Globe* wrote he had a collapsed lung. The *Herald* wrote he had a punctured lung. Channel 4, the CBS affiliate, reported he was close to having surgery.

Dr. David Berger and Dr. Andrew Warshaw revealed that Bledsoe suffered a pneumothorax and that he had not sustained a concussion. They said Bledsoe had a sheared blood vessel in the lining of his lung, which created a condition called a hemothorax in which blood enters the lungs.

"It's a very unusual injury," said Dr. Berger. "I don't think I've ever seen anything like it." While experts in the field of concussions had expressed their views that in their opinion Bledsoe had indeed suffered a concussion, team doctor Bert Zarins would only use the word *stunned* to describe Bledsoe's state after the hit.

Bledsoe said he felt "fuzziness" and then admitted, "Probably in half the games I've played in there's been a little fuzziness. If all the guys came out of the game after being dinged, there wouldn't be a game."

Bledsoe was "The Franchise" for the longest time. In 1993 when he was drafted first overall out of the University of Washington, Parcells was said to be contemplating Bledsoe and Notre Dame's Rick Mirer, until Parcells made his decision to go with Bledsoe. Parcells' fondness for Bledsoe increased after he left the Patriots, and even during the season, when Parcells was cohosting a national radio program with Will McDonough, he referred to Bledsoe as a top-five quarterback in the NFL.

In the midnineties, Bledsoe brought great hope to a franchise that needed a lift. Though the gruff old coach and the young gunslinger sparred at times, the coach understood what he had. Parcells had run a fairly conservative offense in his Super Bowl years with the Giants, but he changed when he realized he had no running game to speak of and a developing offensive line. He allowed Bledsoe to throw more passes for more yards than any young quarterback in the history of the game.

In his first eight seasons, Bledsoe led the Patriots on 19 game-winning drives, 17 of them come-from-behind victories. The greatest of these occurred on November 13, 1994, when he single-handedly reversed a 20–0 deficit late in the first half against the Minnesota Vikings, turning it into a 26–20 overtime win. Bledsoe completed an NFL-record 45 passes of an NFL-record 70 attempts for 426 yards and three touchdowns.

In 1995, Bledsoe broke the team record for most passes (179) without an interception. He eclipsed a 100 quarterback rating 23 times in his first eight seasons, and the Patriots were 22–1 in those games. Bledsoe also made the Pro Bowl three times and led the Patriots to a Super Bowl appearance against the Green Bay Packers in Super Bowl XXX.

Despite two down seasons in 1999 and 2000, when he was sacked 100 times, Bledsoe received a 10-year, $103 million deal on March 7, 2001. The Patriots tiered the contract, the main segment being for four years at $30 million, which included an $8 million bonus. Bledsoe, for appearing in two regular-season games and the AFC championship win, earned $11.5 million.

It was well earned based on his dedication and commitment to the organization. He has always been the perfect superstar for the Patriots. He is friendly, a father of three, and exudes all of the good qualities the Kraft family had hoped for in their superstars.

In 1996 Bledsoe founded the Drew Bledsoe Foundation, dedicated to improving the lives of children through its Parenting with Dignity program, which is run by Mac and his wife, Barbara.

From the time the off-season began in early February until the beginning of March, the Drew Bledsoe Foundation received close to 6,000 e-mails from well-wishers concerning Drew's plight and his future with the team.

It was this wonderful persona that Belichick's decision affected.

Of course, tough decisions were not a new phenomenon for Belichick. His decision in 1993 to go with Testaverde over Bernie Kosar was well documented. Kosar was a hero in Cleveland who had performed well in the late eighties. Belichick came aboard in Cleveland in 1991. Two years later, his relationship with Kosar had declined and Belichick signed Testaverde.

That decision proved fruitful as well. Testaverde led the Browns to a strong 11–5 campaign in 1994, and they beat Bledsoe and the Patriots in the wild-card playoffs that season.

Belichick said that he saw no parallel to the Kosar situation. It's true that Bledsoe was injured and the Patriots had to turn to their backup quarterback, which happened to be Brady, who had beaten

Huard for the job in camp. But it was a case of a younger quarterback taking over for the entrenched incumbent.

"It wasn't popular," said Belichick of his Cleveland call. "Organizationally, I made the decision. Everyone was aware of it in Cleveland. We can all make our judgments on that. I think you have to put the team first, and I did."

Belichick, not afraid to make decisions all season, said, "You're going to be criticized no matter what you do. I just think that's the job. You have to make decisions that aren't popular. If it's fourth-and-1, half the people in the stands want you to go for it, the other half don't want you to go for it. Whichever way you decide, you're going to make people angry. At that point, I'm paid to make decisions. I'll make them."

Belichick said, "We're talking about a released player [Kosar]. With Drew we're talking about a player who did everything he could possibly do to get back to playing from a serious injury. Drew, through no fault of his own, hasn't had the opportunity to play. That's the decision. He hasn't played. Nobody worked harder."

When *Hartford Courant* reporter Alan Greenberg editorialized that Belichick's relationship with Bledsoe had soured, the coach said, "I don't agree with that." However, Belichick did admit later, "I wish I could have done that differently."

Cox, of course, had something to say about Belichick's decision, and it wasn't flattering to Belichick's critics, even accusing the media of trying to undercut the coach.

"You have to support the team," said Cox. "You have to support the decision the guy makes. There would never be a controversy like this in another town."

That was subject to debate.

"Some of the people up here are not capable of making the choice of who should be the quarterback," continued Cox. "They don't know. They don't see the tape."

For Brady, this was just business as usual. He had been in quarterback controversies throughout his tenure at Michigan. Bledsoe was merely Brian Griese and Drew Henson reincarnated from the days when he fought for the right to start. For this stretch of time, anyway, and perhaps for the long-term, this was Brady's team.

What was most bothersome about the Bledsoe situation was that fans and media took sides. Either you were for Brady and against Bledsoe or vice versa. In the off-season, Bledsoe did not attend the victory parade in Boston after the Super Bowl, electing instead to go to Montana with his wife and three children. Bledsoe was criticized, even called a crybaby by some. And when others, speaking for him under the guise of anonymous quotes, said Bledsoe didn't want to play in Cincinnati, which was interested in making a trade for him, he again received criticism. Yet, Bledsoe had not said a word from the moment he left New Orleans to that time.

Sometimes Boston sports fans have short memories. They like to kick their heroes out of town. Some of that was taking place, but for the most part, Bledsoe's fans appreciated and respected his nine seasons in New England.

CHAPTER 16

Thanks for the Keys, Dad

When you talk about everything falling into place for the Patriots, it was never more evident than on November 25 when Brady, given the keys to the car by Belichick, went out and threw four touchdown passes in an emphatic 34–17 win over the Saints.

The Saints, 5–4 at the time, were considered one of the toughest, most bad-ass teams in the NFL. When you played these guys, your body felt as if it went through a meat grinder. You knew you'd be sore the next day. But the Patriots had shown to be pretty tough and physical on their own, and by the time this one was over, the Saints were the ones licking their wounds.

The official dawning of the Brady era was something to behold.

Belichick could have stood at the podium following the victory and said, "I told you so." After all, he had received some criticism for his decision to give Brady exclusivity at the quarterback position, but that was yesterday's news to this coach. Instead he smiled, wished his son Brian a happy birthday, and said, "I thought they played their best football game as a team. I thought the offensive line did an admirable job against a good front."

Brady knew he needed to make a statement about his No. 1 status, and he did it on the field.

"There were about 30 questions at the press conference Wednesday on that subject," reflected Brady. "That's part of it. You learn to deal with it. It's a distraction in that it takes your focus away from preparing for the game each week. If you play bad then it gives everybody an excuse and it's worse the next week and worse the next week. I learned that lesson."

It was indeed a game the Patriots won in the trenches. The line allowed Brady time to throw, and he did that impressively, throwing for 258 yards, four touchdowns, and no interceptions as the Patriots rolled up 432 net yards, 191 of them on the ground.

Brady took advantage of the Saints' man-to-man coverage, and Brown, Edwards, Charles Johnson, and Smith all caught touchdown passes.

"They kept talking about how physical they were," said Patriots linebacker Tedy Bruschi with a look of disgust on his face. "Well, they can keep talking about it on the plane ride home."

It's true. The Saints talked trash throughout the game. Patriots players were surprised at how cocky the Saints were.

Running back Smith gained 111 yards and scored two touchdowns, one on a 41-yard screen pass from Brady, the first receiving touchdown of Smith's career. Screen passes had been a dirty word around New England for a few years, because the team could never execute them properly. Because Bledsoe was such a downfield passer it was like Kentucky Fried Chicken making hamburgers.

Weis, as creative with a playbook as Emeril is with a cookbook, tried a direct handoff to Faulk for seven yards. The Patriots were running well; three times in the previous four weeks Smith had gained more than 100 yards, and the Patriots had won all three games. The play-action passing was also superb. This was right out of the textbook.

The defense stuffed the Saints' ground game, holding Ricky "Don't Lose That Number" Williams to 56 yards on 15 carries.

By halftime it was 20–0.

The Saints scored 10 unanswered points in the third quarter. Despite a momentary shift in momentum, Brady got it back quickly late in the third and early in the fourth quarter when he directed an 80-yard drive, which included another direct snap to Faulk for 24 yards and a 19-yard toss to Brown. Brady used some of his athleticism for a five-yard scramble to the 2, and from there he tossed to Edwards for the score, making it 27–10.

The rest was garbage time, something the Patriots didn't have too much of during the course of this incredible ride.

Now the Patriots were 6–5, trailing the Jets and Dolphins, who were 7–3. They were a team on the rise. You could sense the confidence building even after the loss to St. Louis where Law made the comment, "I think we know we're a good team. I think we know we're capable of playing with anybody and beating anybody on any given Sunday."

The Patriots headed into the crucial month of December touting themselves as a team to watch. This was so different from the previous December. They were speaking in unison about "controlling our own destiny."

The locker room got looser, but the intensity on the practice field was getting greater.

"We're not just playing for pride this December," said Law.

The Patriots' transformation had come full circle. They were no longer laughingstocks, pushovers, or frauds. They were suddenly thrust as legitimate contenders. Belichick was receiving much praise nationally for his coaching, and already he was being talked about as a possible Coach of the Year candidate.

The Patriots had a chance on December 2 to reinforce their newfound respect against the Jets at the Meadowlands. The last time these teams played, everything about the game was ugly. The outcome then was a 10–3 Jets win in which the Patriots committed unsightly turnovers that essentially took them out, and we know what happened to Bledsoe.

Cox, semihealed and ready to play again in a rather miraculous recovery from a broken leg, emphasized to the media that he predicted way back in training camp that the Patriots would be a winning football team.

"If it's a surprise that we're doing what we're doing, it's not to us," said Cox.

With six wins the Patriots had already surpassed the 2000 Patriots. But if they were to finish, say, .500 now, it would be disappointing.

The sportswriters were playing that schedule game again. It seemed as though the Patriots could beat the Jets and the Browns and even the Bills again. The Dolphins could be tough, but the Panthers were thought to be a pushover. The thinking had changed. Now, anything short of 10 wins would be surprising, almost disappointing.

* * *

Between the Saints and the Jets games Glenn was suspended for "conduct detrimental to the team" after the embattled wide receiver refused to practice after being cleared by the medical staff. He was photographed on the field with a cell phone attached to his ear. No pads, no helmet, wearing gray sweatpants and a sweatshirt. Belichick was pictured asking him to go get his gear, and Glenn asked Belichick to have someone get the gear for him.

"It's been six weeks since the injury and he's gotten better," said Belichick. "It's a disciplinary matter; it's not injury-related."

Glenn disagreed with the medical staff's diagnosis. He said, "When I rush back, I aggravate it."

By now Glenn's presence or absence was a footnote. One of the great things about the team was they never allowed the Glenn incidents to disrupt the flow, and this one was no exception.

In fact, Glenn's calamities took the attention away from the rest of the team. The media was so busy writing about Glenn that they'd leave the rest of the players alone, which is precisely the way the coaches and the players like it. Many times players like the media only when they use them for salary purposes. Not all of them, but surely it happens.

Before the Jets game, the *Globe's* Bob Duffy caught up with Mo Lewis, a quiet guy who doesn't often speak to the media. For weeks everyone was wondering how he felt about injuring Drew.

He told Duffy, "I called Bryan [Cox] to wish Drew well and tell him I hoped to see him back on the field. Bledsoe is actually taller than I am. It was just one of those blows. I never thought he'd be injured like he was. I never thought he'd be in the position he's in."

* * *

The Patriots started quite flat. Down 13–0 at the half, in what was being hailed the most meaningful December game in years, the Patriots rallied with 17 second-half points to nip the Jets, 17–16.

The 7–5 Patriots now trailed the Jets by half a game and the 8–3 Dolphins by one and a half games. If the season ended then, the Patriots would have made the playoffs.

What a difference between the two games.

"We're 7–5 and a lot of people didn't think we'd be in this position," said an emotional Belichick, who was 0–3 against his old team prior to the win. "We came from a long way back, a long way uphill, and that's pretty satisfying."

Belichick was hugging players and coaches and giving high-fives and slaps on the back. Phifer was taken aback when Belichick embraced him after the game because he'd "never gotten one of those from him before."

The Patriots were resilient. Down by almost two touchdowns at halftime in the Meadowlands against a 7–3 team isn't the best feeling in the world.

Belichick told the team at halftime, "Our season is on the line. Either we get it done the last 30 minutes, or we're looking down the barrel of the New York Jets."

Cox, who played in his first game since breaking his leg against the Broncos on October 28, called it "the tale of two halves. They controlled the first half, and we controlled the second half."

The Patriots and Brady couldn't muster much against the Jets defense in the first half. The offense converted only one of six on third down. "We just didn't move the ball," said Brady, who finished the day 20 for 28 (15 for 17 in the second half) for 213 yards.

They didn't move the ball because the Patriots were trying to go downfield too much and the Jets' quick pass rushers were coming in on Brady. Weis made a key halftime adjustment when he got Brady to go more to a three-step drop, shortening the range of passes.

The Jets went for the jugular early against the Patriots, as Testaverde threw three of his first four passes down the field, 33 yards to Santana Moss and 34 yards to Laveranues Coles on a slant on which he outran Law and Jones for a 7–0 lead.

John Hall kicked two field goals, but on a 19-yarder the Patriots stuffed the Jets at the 2-yard line as the middle of the Patriots defense dropped Curtis Martin for no gain. That turned out to be a huge defensive stand considering it was a one-point victory.

The Patriots started the second half with defense setting the tone. The unsung Brandon Mitchell tipped a Testaverde pass at the line of scrimmage and the ball was picked off by Vrabel.

Shortly thereafter, fans got an introduction to Fred Coleman, who produced one of the many watershed, unexpected moments of the season.

Formerly cut by the Jets, Coleman caught a 46-yard slant from Brady, which set the stage for Smith's run for a touchdown.

"It was my first pro catch, and I was just excited that I had the chance to contribute to the win," said Coleman, who at age 26 was a study in perseverance, having been cut by four teams.

Hall's 50-yard field goal with 6:37 remaining in the third quarter was the final Jets score.

The Patriots went right back to their trademark short passing game. Brady dumped it off to Smith, who found 40 yards of open territory to the Jets' 27. Weis went to a more change-of-pace running game to give Smith a rest, and Faulk did some nice running inside the red zone before Edwards busted it in from the 4-yard line with 2:11 remaining in the third quarter to make it a 16–14 game.

Vinatieri nailed a 28-yard field goal with 6:29 remaining to give the Patriots the lead for good.

Then it was the defense's turn. As Phifer, who led the defense with nine tackles, four of them behind the line of scrimmage, said later, "We played like there was no tomorrow."

It was a classic bend-but-don't-break moment.

First Jones caused a tough collision with returner Craig Yeast at the 25.

Testaverde, a cool veteran, had plenty of time. He had converted a pair of first downs to the Patriots' 45 with 2:54 remaining. On third-and-5, Matt Stevens blitzed, forcing Testaverde out of the pocket to dump the ball. The Jets decided to go for it on fourth-and-5, but Buckley stepped in front of tight end Anthony Becht to intercept the pass.

All Brady needed to do was run out the clock. Brady had been injured a tad when he bruised his ribs on a hit earlier in the second half. It was third-and-2 at the Patriots' 41 with 1:46 remaining.

Brady came over to the sideline and heard his number called on a keeper, but he questioned Belichick as to whether the team might be better off handing off to Smith. He got this advice from Bledsoe, who put his arm around him and hollered into his helmet grid, "Just run the ball, get the first down, and win the game."

Brady listened to his elder. He got the first down and took three straight knees to run off the clock.

"That was the game I thought put us into a frame of mind that all things were possible," said Kraft. "The San Diego game and this game were the ones, in my mind, that got us to the Super Bowl."

* * *

Suddenly the playoffs no longer seemed impossible.

Shaughnessy wrote in his column in the December 4 *Globe*, "Super Bowl Patriots. There. I said it. None of this fraidy cat, maybe-playoff talk for me. The 2001 Patriots are a team of destiny. They are Super Bowl–bound . . ."

Shaughnessey admitted he was the second media type to say it. The first was Andelman on his daily talk show the previous day.

Even the focused Belichick was getting into it. Maybe he wasn't daring enough to say his team was going to make the Super Bowl, but he said, "When the team was 1–3 I asked them, 'How many wins will it take to make the playoffs?' They answered 10. We had 12. You do the math."

Belichick admitted, "Very early we were a team that lacked confidence. Well, I wouldn't say we lacked it, but we didn't have as much as we do now. We lacked execution. If you go back to the last Jets game and compare it to this Jets game, it's pretty noticeable."

Pretty noticeable, too, was the fact the Patriots would have Glenn back against the Browns. Glenn met with Belichick on December 5 after sitting out the Jets game after the one-game suspension. He walked into Belichick's office at 5:30 P.M. that day.

"We talked about some things and basically we came to the conclusion that I was going back out there," said Glenn. "I'm nervous about it. I really want to be a part of the team, I really do. I don't want to let anybody down. I want to continue to help this team win. They're doing some good things. I'm not going to jump the gun, but I don't want to be a distraction and mess up."

As it turned out he didn't mess up. He caught four passes for 67 yards in a 27–16 win over the Cleveland Browns at Foxboro Stadium on December 9.

Glenn was booed after his first catch, but the boos turned to a mixed reaction by the fourth stanza.

The Patriots were really into this "one game at a time" mode.

"One step closer, one step closer," said Antowain Smith.

"One week at a time," said Kraft, who was beginning what would be many handshakes and waves to his adoring fans at Foxboro Stadium.

"One slip and we're sitting home in January," said Law.

The 8–5 Patriots were certainly well grounded after this win. The Patriots had been motivated by some comments made by Browns players last season after they'd upset the Patriots in Cleveland.

"They're big talkers," said Law, "and the quotes we heard from them after last year's game, we didn't appreciate them. We knew they didn't respect us. They were boasting about beating the Patriots. That's not good."

Bruschi took last season's loss to heart calling it "the worst feeling I ever had on a football field. I really wanted to right the wrong we had there last year and sort of settle some family business."

There you go.

It was these little themes that stuck in their heads and motivated them. Football is a physical game, but it's also a mental game. Psychological ploys can get a team playing to its optimum level, and Belichick and the Patriots played every one of those games.

They also played the physical game so well.

Belichick asked Vinatieri, a former Amsterdam Admirals punter, to fake a 53-yard field-goal attempt and pooch punt in the final quarter, when they were leading 20–16. The ball landed, of course, near the goal line, where Wiggins put his large body in front of the ball as Paxton downed it at the 2-yard line.

"We worked on that play in practice all week," said Belichick. "It's the last play we practice. It's usually well executed by Adam in practice, sometimes not as good as the 1-yard line, but pretty effective. Jermaine did an excellent job to down it."

Vinatieri said, "What you're hoping for is that it lands around the 15 and it gets rolling. I didn't hit a pretty ball, and I was just hoping that it would stay in there. I thought I had a chance, but you never know."

Bad field position for the Browns led to good field position for the Patriots after Troy Brown returned the punt 20 yards to the Cleveland 36 with 6:04 to play. Smith, who ran for 71 yards, got some big yardage on this game-clinching drive, running a pitch left 18 yards and then scoring from 5 yards with 2:49 remaining.

The Browns had led in this one, 10–3, with 1:02 left in the first quarter when Browns corner Corey Fuller returned a Brady interception 49 yards for the score after Vinatieri and Phil Dawson, a former Patriot who had been cut in camp the year before, traded 54- and 27-yard field goals respectively.

Brady, so poised for his age, was not deterred. He made a mistake, but he followed it with a positive, converting four first downs on a drive that began at the Browns' 34. Belichick again made a gutsy call on fourth-and-1 from the 3-yard line when he sent Smith off right tackle. He made two yards for the first down and then went in from the 1-yard line, tying the score at 10 with 9:39 remaining in the first half.

Big plays?

Brown caught seven passes for 89 yards and, before the end of the first half, returned a punt 85 yards when he got two big blocks, one from Milloy on linebacker Dwayne Rudd and another when massive Seymour steamrolled punter Chris Gardocki.

Steady, Brown was clearly one the best players on the Patriots squad, called "Mr. Reliable" by Law. After nine years of struggling to make it as the No. 1 receiver, Brown was still returning punts, playing special teams, and feeling good. "I love doing it," said Brown.

Brown never forgot how hard he fought to make it big in the NFL. He never forgot that returning punts was his bread and butter, until he was discovered as a big-play receiver.

With 85 catches to this point, a career high, Brown was as determined as anyone on the team. A quiet leader whom everyone respected and who led by example, Brown always took it upon himself to make a big play when the team needed it most. So many of his teammates adopted that stance during the course of the season.

When Belichick handed out that "Wanted: Winners" T-shirt in camp, he meant Troy Brown.

CHAPTER 17

Rules Rule

It's tough to resist the pun, but with an 8–5 record, some thought the Patriots were playing unconscious. Well, one of them was, literally.

If Patten hadn't lost consciousness after an overtime reception on December 16 at Ralph Wilson Stadium in Orchard Park, New York, on Fred Smerlas Day, the Patriots may not have beaten the Bills, 12–9, in OT.

Let me digress.

First, football rules are a wonderful thing. They exist to give the officials something tangible to follow so there won't be interpretations like the strike zone in baseball. But some of these rules are dumbfounding. Uh, drop the . . . "founding" part.

Nevertheless, no team benefited more from the rulebook than New England.

It was Rule 3, Section 20, Article 2, Paragraph C to be exact that enabled the Patriots to eke out their ninth and fourth straight win of the season.

Patten caught a pass at about the Bills' 41 in the overtime period when defensive back Keion Carpenter came up on Patten full steam and just clobbered the former sack-of-beans carrier. The little receiver was laid out flat on the field; his head was out of bounds and his torso and legs inbounds. After the hit, the ball lay around Patten's legs inbounds, gathered by Bills defensive back Nate Clements.

It looked like a fumble, felt like a fumble, probably would have tasted like a fumble, but, thanks to the rule, it wasn't a fumble.

Patten, as he would admit later, was out cold, for about 10 seconds in fact.

With the discretion to review the play on his own in overtime, referee Mike Carey opted to review.

"On the play, there is a reception by the receiver [Patten]. He fumbled. The ball was loose in the field of play and while in contact with the receiver's calf, his head hit out of bounds. By rule, that's a loose ball. If a loose ball touches anything that is out of bounds, it is itself out of bounds and it would be in possession of the receiver."

In a nutshell, folks, because Patten's head was lying unconscious out of bounds and because the ball was touching his body, the ball was considered out of bounds as well.

Dead ball. The last person in possession? Mr. David Patten, thank you.

Pretty good rule . . . for the Patriots.

"I knew I caught the ball," said Patten, "but I was out cold for about 10 seconds. When I came to, I saw the replay on the scoreboard. I didn't think we were gonna get the ball back."

What was ironic about the call by Carey was that the officials, who normally tour the camps in the summer to apprise teams of new rules and things to watch for, had come to Smithfield in early August, and, lo and behold, one of the plays they showed was precisely what happened to Patten.

"Yeah," recalled Patten. "They showed us a similar play. Who would think we'd actually live it during the season?"

Ah, fate.

In the previous 41 seasons of their existence, this would not have turned out so well for New England. The call would have gone against them, trust me. The Patriots would have lost this

Kicker Adam Vinatieri (No. 4) reacts to his line-drive 45-yard field goal through the uprights during a driving snowstorm in a playoff win over Oakland.

Tom Brady begins to heat up late in New England's overtime win over the Oakland Raiders in a driving snowstorm at Foxboro Stadium.

"The Call" will forever go down as one of the most controversial plays in NFL playoff history. What looked and felt like a fumble was called a forward pass, which gave the Patriots new life in a game they went on to win in overtime.

Kicker Adam Vinatieri (No. 4) knew he hit the Super Bowl–winning field goal right on the money, as he began to celebrate the Patriots' Impossible Dream win over the Rams.

Ty Law (No. 24) is carrying Otis Smith (No. 45) piggyback as the two Patriot starting cornerbacks, who played superbly against the slippery, fast Ram receivers, celebrate their accomplishment.

Drew Bledsoe looks up to find his family after the Patriots beat the Rams. It was a bittersweet day for Bledsoe; traded to the Buffalo Bills in April, he would never wear the Patriot uniform again.

Lawyer Milloy was the heart and soul of the Patriots' defense. Here he's holding up the No. 1 after the Patriots beat the Rams in the Super Bowl.

Patriot Pro Bowlers (from left) Ty Law (No. 24), Troy Brown (No. 80), Lawyer Milloy (No. 36), and Tom Brady (No. 12) share a victory dance during Media Day in New Orleans.

The streets of Boston are lined with an estimated 1.25 million fans in subfreezing temperatures to greet the Super Bowl champions.

game whether it was the Patriots of the sixties, seventies, eighties, or nineties.

Something special was unfolding before our eyes. Whether we chose to see it was another story.

The fact is, the Patriots retained possession at Buffalo's 41.

Buoyed by the ruling, Antowain Smith, returning to Buffalo for the first time since he was cut in June 2001, put the nail in the Bills' coffin when he rambled for a 38-yard gain to the 3. Talk about great timing! Smith did his usual stunt of breaking away from a pile at the line of scrimmage and busting loose.

"It was just one of those things," said Smith. "I got stopped in a pile of people, my legs kept moving and bounced away. You never give up. I hadn't contributed like I wanted the entire game."

The run set the stage for Vinatieri's game-winning field goal from 23 yards.

Defensively, both teams were stingy.

Vrabel, the former pass-rushing defensive end from Ohio State, had a big game at outside linebacker with eight tackles. He defended three passes as the 4-3 alignment the Patriots had now gone to was stifling quarterback Alex Van Pelt and the Bills' running game.

"It's all about minimizing points," said Milloy. "We're not the No. 1–rated defense, but we're resilient. When it gets down into the red zone, we keep the points off the board."

Offensively, Brady went 19 for 35 for 237 yards, and for the third straight game he hadn't thrown for a touchdown. He was sacked five times, two of them by young defensive end Aaron Schobel, who seemed to get the best of Light. A blitzing Clements hit Brady so hard that his helmet spun off his head and landed seven yards behind him. The Bills, despite their soon-to-be 1–12 record, had come to play.

Otherwise, this was mostly a game of field-goal kickers who excelled on an unusually dry and fairly warm-for-Buffalo winter's day. Certainly it was a far cry from December 2000 when the Patriots won in a blizzard.

The Patriots went up 6–0, but the Bills cut the gap to three in the third quarter after Smith fumbled at the Patriots' 30 when Raion Hill stripped the ball. That set up a Shayne Graham field goal from 41 yards.

"The key to winning games in the NFL is red-zone defenses," said Vrabel. "Make them kick field goals after they drive the ball down your throat. Then you've got something to show for it. Maybe you got your butt kicked, but you gave up three instead of seven."

Vrabel pretty much summed up the key to Patriots defense. It took them to the world championship. In fact, in the Patriots' last five regular-season games, they allowed opponents 10 drives into the red zone and only one touchdown was scored.

The Patriots did have one scare in the game when Law, defending a pass intended for Eric Moulds, came down on his neck. Law felt his spine tingle and things go numb for a few seconds, but all feeling came back. Milloy convinced him to sit out the rest of the game.

Late in regulation, the Bills coaching staff had a brain cramp. What else could you call it? Alex Van Pelt, once the third-string quarterback behind Doug Flutie and Rob Johnson and now the starter, led them on a long, productive drive that ate up 7:46 and 15 plays of the fourth quarter. They drove from the 17 to the Patriots' 7 when Van Pelt took a shot in the far-left corner of the end zone to Peerless Price. It wasn't obvious whether Price had both feet inbounds. The refs called it out of bounds. It was a close call, but the Bills never asked for a replay. "With the [camera] shots we got, we didn't feel it was conclusive enough to overturn the call," said Bills coach Gregg Williams.

But don't you try?

The Bills settled for the tying field goal. The team exchanged two other fourth-quarter field goals to make it 9–9 after regulation.

Then came The Rule.

The Patriots were fortunate to leave Orchard Park (1) without a blizzard and (2) with a win.

* * *

While there was plenty of controversy on the field that week, the days leading up to the game were extremely quiet for the first time all season. It made a person wonder, hmm, they've got this far with all of these little annoyances, how will they react to normalcy? The quarterback controversy was over. Glenn was back, at least temporarily. The team was getting healthy. Football was the focus.

The locker room was always upbeat, but now there was a real sense of urgency and a feeling of what was ahead.

At a small card table near the shower the daily dominoes games were filled with competitiveness of another kind. These guys really went at it in those games. There were even satellite games; usually Charles Johnson and Glenn had their own game going on near their lockers, where the receivers hung out.

Otis Smith had turned the Patriots on to the game, and there were daily tournaments involving mostly the receivers and defensive backs. The games got so intense, there were times players would wait until the last possible moment trying to finish before they headed to practice. If a reporter was looking for a story and the guy he needed was participating in a game, he better quickly turn to Plan B because there was no chance of extracting one of those guys from that table.

The cerebral times continued after the Buffalo game and in preparation for their divisional showdown against the Dolphins at Foxboro Stadium. The feeling was, beat Miami to win the division and then polish off Carolina to host a playoff game.

There was also the possibility the team was about to play its final game at Foxboro Stadium. The old joint saved football in this region back in 1971 because at the time there was a real threat the team could move out of town, possibly to Birmingham, Alabama.

As it turned out, the Patriots hosted Oakland in the divisional playoff game on January 20, but with Miami coming to town there were reflections and memories of the old place.

Not warm, fuzzy ones, however.

In Boston, the Garden had the parquet floor. Fenway had the Wall. Foxboro Stadium had . . .

I asked Jonathan Kraft, is there something of the old stadium that could be brought to the new CMGI Field? Something? Anything?

"We're trying to think of something that we can keep as memorabilia from Foxboro Stadium," said Kraft. "Nothing really stands out right now, but it's something we'll think about."

Of course, the item the majority of people thought about was the toilet flushes. This was in reference to the great story about the first day Foxboro opened, when none of the toilets would flush, creating one messy, smelly day.

The old stadium, which had allowed the Patriots to stay in this area back in 1971, came tumbling down within three weeks after the Super Bowl victory, save for the administration building that housed the draft in April and was the last area to be demolished. The demolition took about three months with all of the phases and the crews having to be careful because of the proximity to the new stadium, which is just a few feet away. It cost about $1.5 million to take it down. Foxboro had been built in 18 months on just less than eight acres, at a cost of just over $6 million.

"We've spent almost four times that in bathrooms at CMGI," said project manager Tim McManus.

The Patriots won environmental awards for the reuse of natural materials at the construction site. The concrete at the old stadium was crushed and used as parking-lot filler. They excavated about one million cubic yards of earth and probably 500,000 tons of rocks and boulders. These were crushed into one-and-a-half-inch and smaller rocks that were used for the slabs, concrete floors, and parking lots at the new place.

There were, however, no "Save Foxboro" groups like the "Save Fenway" groups that called for the refurbishing of Fenway Park rather than a new facility altogether.

"If it wasn't for this stadium, we wouldn't have football in New England. The team would have moved," said Kraft. "Our family sat

in section 217 throughout my childhood in the seventies and eighties, and we have the greatest memories of Foxboro Stadium and the
great games that were played there. We experienced moments we
had as a family that we'll never forget. So, there is a lot of emotion
for our family, and I'm sure the families who have been in this building for years as season-ticket holders. They'll all remember great
times and keep with them their own special memories about it."

* * *

All of the Patriots' energy was directed toward Miami. This was the
team that had beaten the Patriots silly at Pro Player Park in week
four, 30–10. But that was in the heat and humidity. Now the Dolphins
were coming up to frigid Foxboro in December. The Dolphins' history was that they didn't like that feeling.

One of the big matchups was Jason Taylor against Light. Taylor
had stirred the pot a bit when he said of Light in their first matchup:
"He had a couple of cheap shots. If I got up and hit him, I would
have gotten flagged and everyone would be writing in the papers
how nasty and dirty I am. I thought he was competing hard, but I
told him I hope that makes you good because I'm kicking your butt."

Light responded, "He really said that? I don't remember anything
like that. He must have been imagining it."

Taylor had a tough week all around, finding himself in a real-life
sack situation when his 42-year-old stepfather, Anthony Taylor,
allegedly pulled a .22-caliber handgun from an ankle holster during
a heated exchange they were having Monday night, December 19, at
Jason Taylor's Davie, Florida, home.

The 6'6", 260-pound Taylor, who had evidence his stepfather was
trying to extort money from him through the mail, pinned him to the
floor and waited for police to arrive.

The Dolphins were coming off a bad game against the 49ers in
which they were shut out 21–0. Quarterback Jay Fiedler was sacked

six times, almost doubling the total against them for the entire season (13 in all).

Cornerback Sam Madison said, "It seems like whenever we get into a big game like this, we seem to lay down and end up being a pretender instead of a contender. If we want to be a contender, we need to find a way to win games like this. We've got to step up as a team and say enough is enough."

It wasn't enough, and the Dolphins remained pretenders.

This game, played on Saturday, December 22, on a cold night where the game-time windchill was 16 degrees, featured heavy doses of Antowain Smith. There was almost a complete role reversal from October 7 when Dolphins running back Lamar Smith ran all over the Patriots for 144 yards. New England's Mr. Smith ran for a career-high 156 yards on 26 carries and a touchdown.

The Patriots won this game, qualifying for the playoffs in the process, with blood and guts.

Jones, who was an emerging star all season, forced two tide-turning fumbles with jarring hits. The Dolphins had three turnovers; the Patriots had none.

Like a prizefighter, Jones said of his role in the defense, "I don't know what the other teams are thinking, but I know what I'm thinking: I'm looking to knock you out."

Brady threw for 108 yards and broke a three-game touchdown drought with a 23-yard touchdown pass to backup fullback Patrick Pass.

The offensive line consisted of five very determined men ready to rip off the heads of the Dolphins' defensive front. Because the Patriots ran so well, they took Taylor completely out of the game and out of his element.

It was an emotional day for Phifer, who in 11 years had never made it to the playoffs. He said afterward, "This was the most important game of my life. It's the first time in 11 years that I'll be going to the playoffs. I can't tell you what that means to me. I can't tell you how I feel right now because it's a feeling I don't think I've experienced."

The message the Patriots sent was this: we can beat any team.

The game marked the return of the entertaining play. Weis was at it again, trying to seize the moment. Jones' first tremendous pop on tight end Jed Weaver after a 19-yard pass play, a fumble recovered by Otis Smith, resulted in a Weis playground play.

Faulk had been a high school quarterback in Louisiana, and was, for all intents and purposes, the team's fourth quarterback. Faulk took a direct snap from center, rolled right, and spotted a wide-open Brady on the left side. The ball floated in the air for what seemed an eternity, but the Dolphins could do nothing but watch as Brady caught it and ran out of bounds at the Miami 20 for a 23-yard gain.

After the season Weis fessed up to how he came across the play.

"My son Charlie. He's eight, and he's mad at me because he said I stole his play and used it in the game," said Weis.

Weis decided, why not? Sometimes football doesn't have to be so much by the book, so structured, so inhibited. Weis made the game fun for his offense, which had hit so many trick plays that season.

"We practiced that play at least once a week," said Faulk. "Charlie told us we might go with it before the game, but I was shocked to hear it called. It came out of my hand like a jump shot. I knew it was there. I just told Tom, catch the ball!"

Smith took over from there, romping 18 yards to the 2. Then, behind 6'6", 305-pound Seymour, the short-yardage fullback du jour, Smith broke the scoreless tie with a two-yard run with just over seven minutes remaining in the second quarter. Smith had already surpassed 100 yards for the day.

He was far from through. On the next drive, Smith found a hole for a 44-yard run on a terrific cutback, surpassing the 1,000-yard mark for the season. Only three plays later, Brady found Patrick Pass for his only touchdown pass of the game.

At this point, it didn't even appear the Dolphins had made the trip to New England.

After Vinatieri hit a 32-yard field goal, making it 17–0, the Patriots got another break when Vinatieri strategically popped the kickoff high in the air, almost the same thing as an onside kick. It was fielded and fumbled by Tommy Hendricks, and Fred Coleman at the Dolphins' 42 recovered it. The Patriots kept it on the ground but eventually settled for a Vinatieri 22-yarder, making it 20–0.

"They were cheating everybody to that side [to the right], and we tried to kind of make it look like we were kicking left, then wrap around and kick it short right, kind of over the guys' heads," explained Vinatieri. "Best-case scenario: he fumbles. Worst-case: they get the ball at the 30."

Steam was coming out of Dolphins coach Dave Wannstedt's head at this point, and he was screaming at his team on the sideline trying to inspire some life. That seemed to trigger a pulse as Fiedler led a minidrive and settled for Olindo Mare's 36-yard field goal before the half ended.

The second half was just a tremendous performance by the Patriots defense.

The Dolphins were revived, but the Patriots defense stopped them at every turn. The defense hadn't allowed a touchdown in 14 quarters before Fiedler connected with Jeff Ogden with a 10-yard pass with 1:28 remaining. Then came the onside kick—Mare's specialty—but it fell into the arms of Coleman, who grabbed it and endured a vicious hit from a truck named David Bowens. Coleman held the ball.

"I figured if I'm going to get hit like that, I might as well catch it," said Coleman. "And he hit me good, right on the ball, so I had to readjust it as I came down."

Little plays like that, which turned out to be big plays, became signature plays for the Patriots.

Take the Dolphins' first drive of the second half, for instance. It was fourth-and-1 at the Patriots' 21 and Wannstedt decided to go for it. Gutsy call. His team was trailing 20–3, but the game was relatively young and he could have settled for three points. He called a dive for Lamar Smith, but waiting for him on the other side of the pileup were Matt Stevens and Bruschi. Squished fish. The Patriots took over on downs.

The call was similar to one Belichick made at the start of the game. The Patriots were on the Miami 10 and trying to set a tone by going for it on fourth-and-1. Antowain Smith took the handoff and was stopped.

"That's one I wish I could have taken back," admitted Belichick.

Then there was Tebucky.

The Dolphins were driving down to the Patriots' 2-yard line with just over nine minutes left in the game. They handed off to Lamar Smith, and there was Jones, who must have had foreign objects in his hand like WWF wrestlers, because he popped Smith, the ball came loose, and the Patriots recovered.

"I saw his face," said Jones. "It looked like he was dazed. I'm just thinking, don't let them score."

After the game, Belichick and his team went around the stadium to thank the fans. They shook hands and pumped fists, and some players even went into the stands to personally thank them for their loyalty.

"On behalf of the organization, we wanted to show our appreciation," said Belichick.

* * *

The 10–5 Patriots, first place in the AFC East, could now relax. They had a bye week in preparation for their season finale against the Carolina Panthers at Ericcson Stadium.

At 4:00 P.M. Sunday, December 23, the Patriots officially qualified for the playoffs when the New York Giants defeated the Seattle Seahawks, 27–24, on a touchdown pass from Kerry Collins to Ike Hilliard with 20 seconds remaining in the game. Seattle's loss meant the Patriots were in.

It was a chance now for players who were a little dinged up to rest and get away from the rigors of the season. Belichick gave the team some time off over Christmas.

On December 30, the Bills upset the New York Jets, 14–9, insuring that the Patriots would host a playoff game. That was distinguished when the Patriots slaughtered the Panthers in their season finale to earn a bye in the wild-card round of the playoffs.

Amazing.

On January 2, Brady was named to the Pro Bowl team for the first time, while Milloy was selected for the third time. Brown was the obvious snub, but Brown and Law were added later as replacements for Oakland's Tim Brown and Charles Woodson, who were injured.

"There are expectations now," said Brady. "I really have to live up to them now and play like a Pro Bowl quarterback every game and every day in practice."

On top of the world, Belichick cautioned his team about the pitfalls of playing the 1–14 Panthers. And there was the usual distraction of Glenn's being left behind and later suspended for the playoffs.

A Boston.com poll indicated that Troy Brown was the team MVP, garnering 7,370 votes—37.3 percent of the votes—to edge out Smith with 30.2 percent and Brady with 22.8 percent. All great choices, and all of them had a hand in the 38–6 win over the Panthers.

Yes, the Panthers were as bad as their record.

On a drizzly, 36-degree day, where it seemed half of the 21,070 on hand were Patriots fans, it was a fun day.

Bruschi said he saw so many fans with Patriots garb and heard so many cheers for the Patriots that "It felt like a home game. Our fans are very passionate about us."

Law and Smith returned interceptions for touchdowns of 46 and 76 yards while Brown, the people's choice, returned a punt 68 yards to pay dirt.

Brady went 17 for 29 for 198 yards with one touchdown and two interceptions. The Patriots allowed 193 yards rushing, but as I wrote that day, "That would be like saying the ice cream was too cold."

A great roar was heard in the locker room before the media was let in. Belichick and some of the players made speeches. There were hugs and happy talk.

Despite the stampede, it was amazing how focused the players remained.

"You can win 16 games in a row and then lose the first game of the playoffs. What good is that? That's why we have to enjoy what we've done for a while and then get to work with the same focus and concentration we've had," said Bruschi.

He added, "From worst to first. That's what we accomplished in the regular season. With winning comes respect. I think we've earned that the hard way. Now we have to be respected for what we do in the playoffs, and that's the biggest form of respect."

On the plane ride home that night, the Patriots needed the Jets to lose so they would get the bye. Some players had portable TVs, but the signal kept fading in and out. The pilot would often update the team over the intercom.

When the pilot announced the final score—14–9 Bills—there was a little turbulence in the air. The plane, comprised of 300-pound men, was shaking as the team erupted with a roar heard to the heavens.

CHAPTER 18

The White Night

Snow was falling pretty intensely by 4:00 P.M., about four hours before the Patriots were supposed to host the Oakland Raiders in a divisional playoff game on January 19 at Foxboro Stadium. Traffic was backed up forever on Route 1. Early tailgaters lit fires and sloshed down beer and stronger liquids to keep warm. The waft of charcoal-burning grills carried the smell of steak, chicken, and shrimp as the snow sputtered down for what would be a long, snowy, frigid night.

Inside the soon-to-be-demolished edifice, the sod was covered with a tarp. Good; at least the field would still be green for the start of the game. But before you could say "Red Auerbach" the grounds crew was out there peeling off the covering, exposing the field to the elements.

Auerbach may have been at his home in Washington, D.C., chomping on his favorite Chinese entrée, but his spirit was in full force, his character played by one Robert Kraft.

Back in the Celtics' dynasty days of the sixties, Auerbach used to turn the hot water off in the visitors locker room so the opponents had to take cold showers—just his way of employing a little psychology.

Kraft knew what he was doing when he pulled back the tarp. He wanted to instill the same dreaded feeling of playing in Foxboro as the Buffalo Bills created with their home field in their heyday when they made it to four straight Super Bowls.

Kraft, a die-hard Celtics fan, wanted to give his team every advantage. He had fought the league for the prime time night game, which he got. When he saw the snowfall, he saw yet another opportunity for his hearty New England players to gain the edge over the dreaded Al Davis Californians.

The Patriots had won three games in the snow at Foxboro, dating back to 1978. Under NFL rules for stadium protocol, the tarp is required to come off two hours before game time, but this removal was long before that.

The field was blanketed with thick snow very quickly. Workers with blowers occasionally came out to clear the yard lines. Firefighters and police officers being honored at halftime that night were practicing their show, and although officially Kraft pointed to this as the reason the tarp had to be removed early, those of us not born yesterday understood what was going on.

Some patrons had thick layers of snow on their jackets, hats, and gloves, but as 72-year-old Don Botieri, who was at the game that night, said, "It really didn't feel cold." The elements certainly didn't deter the festive mood, which would peak into yet another blissful Patriots moment.

The scene was something out of a Lions-Packers game at Lambeau Field in the midsixties. Actually, other than the cage on the helmets as opposed to one bar, you really couldn't distinguish the modern design of the uniforms.

In the final game ever played at Foxboro Stadium, the old joint didn't look much different than it did in its infancy 31 years earlier—gray, aluminum seating and concrete slabs covered with snow.

The last significant time the Patriots had seen snow in a big game was December 12, 1982. In that game Mark Henderson, who was working the snowplow that night as part of a work-release program from a local prison, was summoned to the field by then-coach Ron Meyer to plow off a spot from which John Smith could boot a game-winning field goal in a 3–0 win over Miami, sending Hall of Fame coach Don Shula into a snit of snits that to this day he has not got over.

The Henderson story was fascinating, almost eerie.

I had made a TV appearance on New England Cable News earlier in the week, and a recent clip was shown of Henderson being interviewed. I turned to host Mark Ockerbloom and said, "That can't be. Mark Henderson is dead. It must be a hoax."

A few years after the snowplow game it was reported in the media that Henderson had passed away of natural causes. Evidently, this wasn't true. More than a decade went by when suddenly, a couple of days before Alumni Day at Foxboro Stadium, Mark Henderson reappeared.

Smith and other players positively identified Henderson. Now living in Rhode Island, Henderson explained that the media had the wrong Mark Henderson back then. The one who died was also an inmate at the same jail. Henderson said he never bothered to correct the report because he didn't want to bring attention to himself.

Was this an omen or what?

* * *

Fans didn't get home that night until well after 2:00 A.M. The parking lot was jammed for hours. The great debate on talk shows even after the game: was it the greatest game ever played at Foxboro Stadium? Part of the game was exciting and wonderful, but early on the game dragged as neither team could get much going in the four or five inches of snow they were playing in.

Even so, it certainly was most entertaining and a great game given the situation, given the fact that it was the final game in Foxboro.

There had been debate about rustiness as a result of two bye weeks in a three-week period. Hard to say if rust had anything to do with the results of a game played in a snowstorm.

It was evident from the outset that neither team would be able to run effectively. If removing the tarp was strategy in favor of the Patriots, it wasn't working out that way. Traction was bad. Running and throwing the ball to the outside weren't working too well. To win they had to have a controlled, short- to middle-range passing game.

Brady went 32 for 52 for 312 yards, 26 for 39 in the second half.

Why so strong in the second half? Dr. Belichick said the game might come down to which team made the best in-game adjustments. Well, truer words were never spoken. After only 74 passing yards in the first half, adjustments were made.

"We tried to do a few things differently in the passing game," said Belichick. "Some of the things we thought we could do against the Raiders weren't going particularly well. We didn't play that well in the first half. We only had a couple of first downs. Charlie and I talked before the game about the Buffalo game [last December in a blizzard]. Even though the schemes were different, conceptually the types of plays we wanted to run were the same. So we said we've got to go back to that, and I think that helped. Give Tom and the receivers credit. They did a good job throwing it and catching it and handling it in those conditions."

The Raiders were up 7–0 at the half. Brady started well in the third quarter as he drove the team down the field on two long passes to Patten for 25 and 19 yards all the way to the Raiders' 9-yard line. But Brady overthrew Patten and Rod Rutledge on two attempts in the end zone, forcing a field goal. Vinatieri hit from 23 yards with 8:39 remaining in the third quarter. Even more impressive was Raider Sebastian Janikowski's 38-yard field goal with 4:14 remaining to make it a 10–3 game.

Later, Janikowski hit from 45, making it a 13–3 game with 1:41 to go in the third quarter.

Down 13–3 in the fourth quarter, Belichick said he and Weis huddled again, and the suggestion was made that it was time to pick up the tempo.

"I think that's exactly what happened. Early in the fourth quarter after our second drive with 12 or 13 minutes left, I told Charlie it's a two-score game. We need to get going, and how about the no-huddle and change the tempo of the offense? That's what we decided to do," Belichick said.

Brady was superb in the no-huddle offense. At one point he completed nine straight passes, four of them to Wiggins, who had 10 catches. Wiggins had 14 receptions in 16 regular-season games. Brady also threw three passes to Patten and one to Faulk before scrambling in from the 6 with 7:52 remaining, making it 13–10.

It was a great moment for Wiggins, a kid who grew up in East Boston watching Ben Coates play tight end as a kid.

"He was like our snowplow," said Belichick.

What stuck out was the way Wiggins caught the icy pigskin as if he'd lived here all his life. Heck, he had.

Wiggins fancied himself more a Charles Barkley–like player for the East Boston High hoop team than a football player, but now he was becoming a hometown hero before our eyes. Wiggins wasn't thrown to much during the season, although he has good hands.

"When they called my number," said Wiggy, "I tried to seize the opportunity and take advantage of every opportunity I can get. That's what I tried to do out there. We just played an all-around team game and when your number's called, you've got to answer."

* * *

The best kick of the game occurred with 27 seconds remaining in regulation play. Vinatieri made the field goal to tie the score at 13, a 45-yard line drive, end-over-end, an as-ugly-as-it-could-get boot through a snowstorm.

"I was trying to get more elevation, but with the condition that was almost impossible," said Vinatieri.

The field goal was set up after a controversial call reversal by referee Walt Coleman, who had called a fumble on Brady after Charles Woodson stripped the ball on a corner blitz. After the review, Coleman, who said "Oh [bleep]!" when he realized he had made the wrong call, ruled that Brady's arm was going in a forward motion, thus ruling that it was an incomplete pass.

"Yeah, I was throwing the ball," grinned Brady at the postgame press conference.

The ruling triggered debate for days. It looked as if Brady dropped back to throw, his arm in forward motion, but then when he knew Woodson was bearing down on his right side, he brought the ball down and patted it with his left hand as he was being tackled.

"Obviously, what I saw on the field, I thought the ball came out before his arm was going forward, but when I got over to the replay monitor and looked at it, it was obvious his arm was coming forward," explained Coleman. "He touched the ball and they just hooked it out of his hand. His arm was coming forward and that makes it an incomplete pass. He would have had to bring it all the way in and then it comes out. Then it would have been a fumble."

Jon Gruden, who left the team to sign a new deal with Tampa Bay in late February 2002, went ballistic. He was beside himself, his arms going in umpteen different directions as he attempted to get some explanation of a call that was unexplainable if you didn't believe the rule.

Gruden said later that he couldn't even watch the play on replay, saying, "When a call like that goes against the team you're coaching, you don't want to spend too much time dwelling on it."

The sidelight: we were all looking for the tucking of the ball, but how about that right arm to Brady's helmet that Woodson delivered prior to the overturned fumble call? Was there not roughing the passer on this play? Shouldn't the Patriots have been 15 yards deeper down the field?

"There was a little incidental contact, but not enough to make a roughing the passer call," said Mike Pereira, director of officiating for the NFL.

Pereira, like everyone else, noticed the contact by Woodson after the fact. Actually, everyone was concentrating on fumbles and forward passes and tucking the ball in. For days Pereira, working at the NFL offices in New York, reviewed the play endlessly and even brought out video of similar plays and similar calls. To this day Pereira remains steadfast that the rule is sound and a much-needed one for officials to be able to use.

The rule was supposed to be reviewed by the competition committee at the owners' meeting in Orlando in March, but when the committee convened prior to the meetings, not one team offered an alternative to the "tuck" rule, and it was again in the books for 2002.

"What the rule says is if the forward motion of the arm continues, even in the process of attempting to tuck the ball back into your body, it's incomplete. If the ball is knocked out of his hands, if he loses it on his own, as long as the ball is not tucked completely into the side of his body, that's an incomplete pass," said Pereira.

What if the quarterback's arm has gone forward, the ball hasn't been released and the left hand is now handling the ball, as appeared to be the case with Brady?

"The ball has to be tucked all the way into the side of your body," said Pereira. "Then if the ball comes out, it's a fumble. Otherwise, it's an incomplete pass. Having reviewed the many plays we have on this call, this is a great rule. If we didn't have this rule, it would be up for the individual officials' interpretation. This way there's a rule, and I think it's a good one."

Pereira said if the arm is recocked and in the passing motion, then if the ball is lost, it's a fumble. If a quarterback has pump-faked and then begins to recock the arm and the ball is lost, that is a fumble. But if he has pump-faked and the ball hasn't been tucked into the side of the body and the ball is lost or stripped, it's an incomplete pass.

At worst it was a borderline call.

"It was a very good call. Under the rule the way it's written, overturning the fumble was the right call," said Pereira, who said that 15 fumbles were overturned and called incomplete passes based on the rule.

The call conjured memories of 1976 when official Ben Dreith called roughing the passer on Patriots defensive end Ray Hamilton, who hit Ken Stabler high, but several replays of the call did not indicate the roughness Dreith saw that day.

"That play was played over and over again that week," said Hamilton, now the defensive-line coach for the Cleveland Browns. "For the longest time, it was just a New England thing. People around the country didn't know much about it. Now they do. I've had a lot of people come up to me and say, 'What a lousy call!' What a tough way to lose a game."

The Dreith call set up the Raiders' winning score and knocked the Patriots out of the playoffs. Many Patriots historians believe that 1976 team may have been the best Patriots team ever in terms of talent, and they probably would have gone to the Super Bowl.

But that was the difference between past Patriots teams and this one. With this one, the breaks went their way.

* * *

Some of the faithful had begun to leave Foxboro after Brady's fumble.

Belichick tells the story: "One of my family members was sitting in the stands, and when we had the fumble, a couple of people jumped up and walked out. By the time the officials replayed it and called it an incomplete pass and awarded us the ball, they came scrambling back to their seats. I'm telling you, the place was full until the end. I would imagine anyone who attended the game would remember it. It was a special one."

While it was important to the outcome that the Patriots had received the benefit of Coleman's review, that didn't seal anything. It only gave them a chance.

The Patriots were in possession of the football with 2:06 remaining and down by three. Brown returned a punt 27 yards to the 46. He fumbled it, but he recovered. The Patriots had no timeouts remaining. The ball was on the 42.

After the call reversal, the score stood at 13–10 and the Patriots still had to move the ball into field-goal range. Brady marched them as far as the 28. It was fourth down, and at that point they'd reached the end of the road. It was time for Vinatieri to do his magic.

"We didn't have any choice," said Belichick. "We had a lot of confidence in Adam to make it. You have to give a lot of credit to [long snapper] Lonie [Paxton] and [holder] Kenny [Walter] for the hold. They were tough conditions."

When Vinatieri's 23-yard field goal with 6:31 remaining in overtime went through the uprights, 60,000 fans went into a frenzy, teammates hoisted Vinatieri, and snapper Lonie Paxton made snow angels in the end zone. The win not only thrust the Patriots into the championship game against Pittsburgh but also into the "Impossible" chapter of their season's story.

The *Globe's* Bob Duffy wrote of Vinatieri, "He had slush at his feet, snow in his eyes, blizzards in the background, and ice in his veins."

Brady had a huge hand in getting them to that spot. Winning the toss for the overtime period, the Patriots elected to receive the ball. Brady, who always seemed to seize these opportunities, completed six straight passes—three to J. R. Redmond and three to Jermaine Wiggins.

Brady advanced to the Raiders' 27 but that wasn't close enough. It was fourth-and-4. With a stiff wind blowing at the kicker's face, Belichick thought the Patriots were better off trying to make the first down than attempting what would have been a field goal of about 43 yards.

Once again, Brady reinforced the coach's decision. He completed a pass to Patten's knees at the 22. The Patriots moved it on the ground with Smith all the way to the 5-yard line.

Eerily, the scoreboard went a little screwy. Even before Vinatieri attempted the final kick, the scoreboard read Patriots 16, Raiders 13.

You just can't make this stuff up.

Gruden tried to freeze out Vinatieri by calling a timeout, but that backfired because it gave Vinatieri and his teammates time to do a bit of snow removal with their feet.

Vinatieri calmly followed through with a perfect kick.

Afterward the Raider locker room was as cold as the outdoor setting they had just lost in.

"You guys make the decision on that," said Jerry Rice, future Hall of Famer. "I feel like we had one taken away from us. It's just unfortunate. We worked hard and I felt we deserved to win this football game."

Even stronger was Woodson, who categorized it as a "bullshit call. It never should have been overturned."

For days the Raiders griped they were robbed. Receiver Tim Brown brought out the Al Davis conspiracy theory that the league was getting back at the Raiders for past transgressions.

"People try to say that what goes on between Al Davis and the league doesn't affect what happens on the field," fumed Brown. "But there's no way that you can tell me that that's so. There's no way that was his throwing motion. I'm sure they're going to review that in the off-season."

The words *luck* and *destiny* were now being thrown around all over when it came to the Patriots. The team of destiny, which had been the seven-and-a-half-point underdog in its own backyard, was moving on to the AFC championship game against Pittsburgh, where, believe me, absolutely nobody thought the Patriots would leave the victors or the spoilers.

*   *   *

Earlier in the day Belichick had lost in the Coach of the Year voting to Chicago's Dick Jauron in a close vote. Jauron had turned the Bears from 5–11 in 2000 to 13–3. Belichick had gone from 5–11 to 11–5.

When Jonathan Kraft tried to console Belichick and tell him he should have won the award, Belichick said, "I don't care about that. We're going to prepare to beat Pittsburgh."

CHAPTER 19

Just a Little Respect

By the time Lawyer Milloy accompanied Belichick and Brady to Pittsburgh for a pregame press conference on January 25, he'd had it with all of the *luck* and *destiny* talk. Vegas had made the Steelers nine-point favorites. Milloy felt nobody was giving the Patriots a modicum of respect for their accomplishments. There was little acknowledgment of the Patriots as a legitimate power-house, and this hurt Milloy's inner being beyond anything any of us could imagine.

Even after the Steelers had beaten the Ravens to host the AFC championship at Heinz Field, coach Bill Cowher instructed his players to get all of their Super Bowl plans out of the way before this game, because he wanted them to concentrate on what was ahead.

Just mentioning "Super Bowl" proved a major motivating tool for the Patriots. Sure, the Patriots also had to make plans, but theirs were being made behind the scenes, not in the open like the Steelers'.

"There's nothing wrong with talking about winning the Super Bowl," said Cowher. "It's not out of disrespect for New England. We know it's gonna be a battle. It's just that we're not afraid to talk about it."

The Patriots were taught by Belichick to respect the opponent. It's not that the Steelers didn't, but by making Super Bowl plans the Steelers gave the impression that they felt they were already in.

To Milloy, respect means everything. In his opinion, the New England Patriots had been disrespected. Poor Steelers. You don't want this guy playing with a head of steam. You know how angry Ray Lewis can get on the field? Milloy can match it.

Before a national audience at the AFC championship press conference, Milloy had predetermined that any questions associated with luck and destiny were going to set him off. He was also getting more and more steamed in the background of the Friday press conference as he listened to Kordell Stewart talk about going back home to play in New Orleans.

When questions began to come up about the Patriots being a team of destiny, Milloy blew, going as far as to say he felt like former heavyweight champion Mike Tyson at that moment. That week, Tyson had gone nutty on stage in a prefight press conference with Lennox Lewis.

"Any competitor plays this game looking for respect," said Milloy. "That's all we're looking for. Right now we don't feel like we're getting that respect. And we're fighting for the AFC championship. And that's crazy to me. I almost feel like Tyson did the other day. He's sitting there at the podium. Lennox Lewis is sitting there at the podium. He's sitting there and he's the former heavyweight champion of the world. And they're saying here . . . Lennox Lewis the former undisputed champion of the world. They're talking about how good he is, and Mike Tyson is sitting over there watching and listening to all of this—just like we're watching Pittsburgh, and all of the teams in the commercials for the playoff teams. Like I said, what about us?

"What did Mike do?" asked Milloy. "He snapped. The only difference is, we're not going to do it [snap] on the podium, we're gonna do it out on the field. We're going to let our emotions fly on the field, and that's what it's all about. It's not about trash talking, it's about the best team is gonna win. We're coming down here to win."

When the *New York Post*'s Kevin Kernan asked about being focused on this game, Milloy had to contain himself.

"Are you kidding me? Are you serious with that question?" said Milloy. "I've got to count to 10. I told myself before I got mad up here with one of those questions. The reality of it is, I'm not here to lose. Our team is not a team of destiny. This team is trying to take advantage of us being a good team. I know the focus is pretty much on the other three teams that have a chance to compete for that trophy at the end of the year. Our focus has always been on us. We haven't let it seep outside of our locker room. We're focused on the direction we're heading in as a team, and that's what makes us good. Go ahead and overlook us all you want. We watch ESPN. We watch the playoff commercials. They have all the other teams on there and I don't see one guy from our team on that commercial. They have guys on that commercial talking about playoff experience and the atmosphere, and it's guys who haven't even been in the playoffs before. That's crazy."

While some of Milloy's teammates had dismissed the "destiny" tag and have used the "lucky" label as a motivator, Milloy was clearly insulted.

Brady was trying to downplay Milloy's comments, but when pressed whether the "destiny" tag insulted him he too chimed in: "To me, when you see 'team of destiny,' to me that means we're lucky to be here. I don't think we're lucky to be here. We're a pretty darned good football team, and we've proved that. If you want to be the best you have to prove that too. People are gonna call you what they want. A 'team of destiny'? I've been called worse than that."

He added, "We're not going to be able to roll our helmets out there and win the game. We're in this situation for a reason. We play hard. We come up with plays when we need them. Offensively. Defensively. Special teams. That's why we're here. If that's destiny, that might be the word to use. There have been times when calls haven't gone our way. We're here because we earned it.

"A lot of people have been saying we're lucky all year," said Milloy. "Destiny. When you win a Super Bowl it is destiny. It's destiny at some point. Are we lucky to be here? No. This is a good team because we don't panic as a team. We were 0–2, and we didn't panic at 1–3. When our record was .500 in the middle of the year, we had to face a lot of teams that we had to beat to get back into the divisional or the conference race. And we did."

Brady talked about the team's short focus on the game at hand. When told the Steelers were talking about the Super Bowl, Brady said, "That's pretty far off in my mind at this point. We're not thinking about the Super Bowl. We're thinking about the Pittsburgh Steelers. That's quite a challenge in itself. If they want to take on the Super Bowl and the Patriots, that's up to them to do."

The Patriots added some of their own spice to the game when Law, speaking to his hometown paper, the *Pittsburgh Tribune-Review*, said that the Patriots needed to get rough and tumble with the Steelers receivers. He didn't say it quite that diplomatically, however.

"I just think they need to be smacked in the face," Law told the newspaper. "That's what we'll give them. If they want to play rough, good, that's my type of game. Bring it. Let's see what you got." Law also spoke of "shredding" Plaxico Burress' confidence. Burress, at 6'5", dwarfed Law, who was 5'10".

Law, after a talk with Belichick, recanted his comments, saying he was misquoted.

"I did nothing to disrespect their football team. My apologies to their team and whoever I so-called attacked. I didn't say anything to disrespect their team," said Law.

Nevertheless, it had created some bulletin-board material for the Steelers, whose motivation was to make it to the Super Bowl.

Certainly, the Patriots had to take on the "Bus" (Jerome Bettis) and Kordell Stewart. They also had to take on the elements at Heinz, which had been a Bermuda triangle for kickers.

As usual, Belichick was building up the opponent so he could take them down.

Said Belichick, "Pittsburgh has as many gadget plays as anybody in the league. The first time I've seen it in 20 years—they ran a triple reverse. Another play I've never seen in 26 years—they ran a play without a quarterback in the game. I've never seen the quarterback not be on the field for a play. They snapped it to Ward. He's a receiver. They've done single reverses, fake reverses, and halfback passes. You name it they've run it. You're going as far back to watch as much as you can. You see more and more, at some point you pick out the ones you're likely to hit."

Maybe it upset Milloy that the Patriots were always underdogs, but it proved to be the biggest motivational tool of the season. All Belichick had to do was point to what the media was saying about them.

"I've been an underdog my whole life," said Cox. "No one gave us a chance to be in this position, and that's fine. I've never let anyone tell me who I am or who I'm supposed to be. If I allowed people to tell me that, I'd be dead or in jail at this time."

Lucky? Sure, what team that has made it this far into the season isn't lucky? Good? Of course they're good. "Any team still playing this time of the year is good," said Bill Belichick.

"Sometimes you can be good and get your butt beat, or you can be lucky and win," said Cox.

Cox hadn't been just lucky; he was good. Here's a guy who played two plays against Oakland. One of them was huge. He stopped Zack Crockett on third-and-1 late in the fourth quarter, after Richard Seymour had moved to left tackle where he got great penetration, and Cox came in to make the hit.

In Cox's opinion, "Everything happens for a reason. If we get a break, hey, it means we've done something to earn it. This team earns everything it gets. Nothing is handed to us. I don't know how anyone could think that if you know anything about our team."

Not many knew about this team because they chose to turn the other way.

In preparation for the game the Patriots tried their best to simulate Kordell in practice. Belichick used Faulk, Huard, and Bledsoe to play the role.

"We don't have Kordell," said Belichick.

Neutralizing Stewart was high atop the wish list, right up there with putting a stop sign on the "Bus."

The Patriots had to blitz a bit, but as Bobby Hamilton pointed out, "If you blitz, you'd better get there because if you don't he can get around you and run down the field."

That's why the big word of the week was *alert.*

The players talked about being alert, expecting anything and everything from not only Stewart but also an offense that can get very imaginative with a host of gadget plays, including plays in which Stewart acts as a running back.

"You definitely don't want him to get outside," said Belichick. "He's fast. He can really run. He's not a guy who can just pick up the first down and then slide. It could be a lot more than six or seven yards when he carries the ball. They have a number of plays . . . where he goes back and the action of the play goes one way, and then he runs a sweep or reverse the other way. The play goes over here, and he goes the other way, but he goes with a bunch of blockers. They have more blockers than you have defenders because you need to match the play on the other side where it started. They also have a couple of plays where he goes up the middle. But most of it is outside stuff. It's like an option. They have one more guy than you have to defend it. It puts pressure on the defense."

Belichick said some teams, such as Baltimore, Jacksonville, and Cleveland, did a good job containing, but they never shut him down.

Would there be a spy on Stewart?

Belichick wasn't about to let the cat out of the bag.

"Kordell has seen a spy since 1995. We saw a play where the Jets tried to spy him, but the problem is, Kordell is faster than the spy. And I think that's always a problem when you put a guy on Kordell or a Randall Cunningham or an Aaron Brooks or a Doug Flutie. There's no point spying with someone who's not athletic. The only guys who run fast enough to get him, you need out there covering

Hines Ward and [Plaxico] Burress and those guys. That's the dilemma," Belichick said.

Bettis had missed the previous six games with a groin pull, but he had led the NFL in rushing with 1,072 after 11 games. The Patriots had always done a decent job against Bettis, holding him to about 60 yards a game and 3 yards per carry in four games.

Bettis had spent the off-season working out with Law in St. Louis at Bob Kersee's conditioning program. Law called Bettis the Tuesday before the game to talk smack and tell him "I hope I can get a few shots at you," which he did.

There was also the distinct possibility the game could come down to kicking, just like the Patriots-Raiders game.

Vinatieri's exploits in bad weather were well chronicled at this point. Now he was asked to perform miracles at Heinz Field.

The south end of the stadium, which is open and faces the river, was thought to have demons hovering around the goal posts. Coming into the game, Kris Brown had missed 10 of his 24 attempts. In all, Brown had missed a league-high 14 field goals (he only missed 4 of his 20 attempts on the road) after missing 9 in two years at the Steelers' old home at Three Rivers Stadium.

Brown did his collegiate kicking at Nebraska, where there was turf, and of course Three Rivers had turf. The Heinz sod had been ridiculed during the year. Charges of footing problems were often raised. Only three kickers had made field goals at Heinz: Matt Stover, Gary Anderson, and Brown.

The Steelers are also first in field-goal defense, if we can make that a category for editorial purposes. Opponents hit only nine regular-season field goals against the Steelers, the fewest in the NFL since 1984.

Brown made two of his three attempts against the Ravens in a 27–10 win on January 20, but he also missed a 35-yarder.

For as much as Brown was considered a liability, Vinatieri was considered an asset. Belichick considered him a "football player" as well as a kicker, a high compliment for any kicker. He takes part in the team's strength and conditioning program and keeps up with all of the positional players.

Vinatieri didn't need to tackle or carry the ball; all he needed to do was make the kick when the team needed it most.

The Patriots hoped it came down to the will of the players, because they had a lot of it.

Law and Milloy were reminded of the disrespect they felt even as they ate their last supper before the game at a local Pittsburgh establishment. Law, who grew up in the suburbs of Pittsburgh, took his mother and Milloy out for dinner. At the end of the meal, the waitress, unaware of whom she was serving, brought over some complimentary "Steelers cookies."

"I told her to get those things away from me," said Milloy.

CHAPTER 20

Rewrite, Please

Hollywood scriptwriters probably would have thrown this story in the reject bin under Not Believable.

It's the story of the fallen quarterback who miraculously returns to lead the team that dissed him to the AFC championship win and a Super Bowl berth? Stuff like that only happens in corny flicks, not in box-office hits.

Amazingly, it happened to the New England Patriots. It happened to Bledsoe. By now a segment of the media and general population had either remained loyal to him or had forgotten him. Either way it was Brady's team.

But for most of one very important game, it was Drew's team again.

In whatever corner you belonged, the comeback was perhaps the biggest feel-good aspect to a feel-good story.

After all was said and done, Bledsoe didn't have to go home to his Montana retreat feeling as if he had only contributed to the bad parts of the season. He returned to Montana with the feeling that he had had his moment, his own special contribution to a 24–17 win over the Steelers, capturing the AFC championship for the first time since 1996.

On a makeshift podium at Heinz Field in the late afternoon of a balmy January 27 day, Bledsoe stood hoisting the championship trophy, pumping it in the air and passing it to his teammates. He fought back tears, and as he moved off the podium he spotted his father, Mac, and they embraced in one special father-son moment.

Bledsoe had been so close to death; now he was so close to a championship that he had a hand in.

"I thought about this moment for months," said Bledsoe. "I've had the dream for weeks. I saw myself in the game. I knew what the plays were. I played them out in my dreams—where to throw the ball, what to look for. I had all kinds of game situations in my dreams. I saw the touchdown pass I threw today. That's why I was excited when the call came in. That's one of my favorite pass routes. The deep corner. I know I can throw that one. And then it came. I saw it coming and I knew what I had to do."

Bledsoe entered the game with 1:40 remaining in the first half.

He hit Patten on a 15-yard pass to the Steelers' 25 for a first down when grave dèjá vu and Bledsoe met.

The big, lumbering No. 11 was forced to run for four yards, and that's where a vision of Mo Lewis appeared. It was really the lighter, smaller Steelers safety Chad Scott who lined up for a big sideline hit, knocking Bledsoe way out of bounds. The officials did not call a flag, for even though Scott left his feet, Bledsoe was not yet out of bounds when the hit occurred.

Bledsoe, who cut his chin on the play, charged back. He was fired up. If there was any wooziness or fuzziness—and there was—he wasn't about to let anyone know. He went right back to work with a 10-yarder to Patten at the 11 and then threw a beauty of a TD pass to Patten in the right corner of the end zone over a defensive back and in front of a linebacker, with 56 seconds remaining.

Four months of inactivity . . . to come in and direct a big touchdown was extraordinary.

"He gets very few reps [in practice]," said Weis. "I'd say he should be proud. That's a pretty hard thing we asked him to do."

"It's one thing to think about these situations and dream about them. It's another thing to go out and do it," Bledsoe said. "You can't freeze when you have the chance. You must be just as aggressive as you were when you played through it in your mind. That's what I told myself today. Don't back off. Make the tough throws. Go after these guys. And I did. I wasn't afraid. I wanted to stay aggressive and we did."

Brady had gone 12 for 18 for 115 yards, facing mounting pressure from linebacker Jason Gildon. The score was 7–3 Patriots late in the first half when Lee Flowers, blitzing from Brady's right side, rolled into the back of his legs, causing an ankle sprain that took Brady out of the game. No penalty was called.

After Bledsoe's heroics, it was 14–3 Patriots at the half, an upset in the making. But even at this point many of those watching the game from the national media perspective did not believe this would be the final outcome.

Asked if Brady could have gone back out there Belichick said, "He [Brady] could have gone back out and played, but I just felt like the way things were going we were better off with a healthy Drew Bledsoe, not knowing where Tom was with his injury."

It was more than Bledsoe.

There aren't many guys who can set the tone for the game at the coin toss, but Cox managed it. The Rehbein family had been brought out to participate in the toss, a nice gesture by the Patriots. But off to one side, the "Bus" started to talk trash, and Cox, a defensive cocaptain, got in his face. It was like a couple of boxers mixing it up before the opening bell.

"I just wanted to make a point that we were not backing down. He started talking about how he was ready and all this and that, and I said 'Jerome, this ain't what you're gonna be looking for today,'" Cox said.

Big-time players, like Bledsoe, make big-time plays. When you think big play you think Troy Brown.

Steelers punter Josh Miller booted a long, 47-yard punt on which Troy Brown shot through the middle of the field. Perfect. All week long in practice the Steelers had prepared to steer Brown to the sideline because they felt he wasn't as effective there. But Brown did his own driving. Along the way Bruschi crushed a Steeler to spring Brown free, giving the Patriots a 7–3 lead with 3:43 remaining in the first quarter.

"It was supposed to be a left return," recalled Brown, who set the championship-game record for most yards per touch, 18.3 yards per touch. "But the guys overplayed it to the outside, and I saw the seam up the middle and we just hit it. It was just a great play by the punt-return team."

An even better play was the one that set it up.

Miller had lofted a 64-yarder that Brown misfielded and allowed to scoot by him to the 23-yard line. But Steelers special teamer Troy Edwards was flagged for running out of bounds and then back in bounds, and officials, who had numerous calls to make early in this one, called the penalty that forced the repunt.

Unnoticed was the veteran Buckley, a very intelligent player, who became a big factor in the postseason ride. He had chased Edwards down the sideline, and his strategic crowding probably caused Edwards to step out.

"It's not something I did by design, but if I can crowd him and make him go out, that's a legitimate call. We got the repunt and Troy did the rest," said Buckley.

Up 7–0, the Patriots had already silenced parts of the full house. But the Steelers finally began to move the ball when Stewart got loose for a 34-yard run after hurdling over a blitzing Milloy in the backfield to get away.

Belichick wasn't happy with this. He had a scowl on the sideline because he had warned his team of Stewart's ability to run.

Two pass completions later, the Steelers were first-and-10 at the Patriots' 13. But the Patriots' tough red-zone defense stiffened as Pleasant sacked Stewart for a two-yard loss. Tough press coverage by Otis Smith on Burress broke up a pass and forced the Steelers to settle for a 30-yard field goal by Kris Brown.

After Bledsoe's heroics brought the Patriots into the locker room with an 11-point lead, the Steelers came out juiced up. Stewart drove the Steelers down to the Patriots' 16 in the third quarter, but they had to settle for a 34-yard field-goal attempt.

Kris Brown, who had made one chip shot but wasn't a huge factor to this point, soon became one. When he went to go through the ball, he found Brandon Mitchell's hands blocking the kick. The ball squirted behind him where Troy Brown, taking Belichick's "be alert" mantra to heart, spotted the loose ball, picked it up, and ran 11 yards before he had the foresight to lateral to safety Antwan Harris for the remaining 49 yards and the score, giving the Patriots a 21–3 lead.

"I saw Antwan coming over my shoulder and he was screaming my name, and from there I just wanted to make sure it was a lateral; and he did a great job. Worked out great for us," said Troy Brown.

Mitchell was screaming and laughing all the way down the field. The seldom-quoted lineman said, "I had so much fun out there."

If you stop and look at the play, it looked an awful lot like a forward pass, but the refs missed it and nobody on the Steelers bench challenged it.

Bettis, playing his first game in seven weeks, was stuffed all day by the Patriots defense with a season-low 58 yards on 22 carries.

"It was just the attitude that we had from the first snap to the last snap. We had the attitude that we weren't going to run the ball against us," said Seymour.

It got to the point where Stewart had to throw the ball to Bettis just to get him more touches.

Two Stewart-to-Bettis passes were 11 and 19 yards, and then Stewart hit Hines Ward for 24 more. The 79-yard drive culminated in Bettis' 1-yard run with 5:11 remaining in the third quarter, making it 21–10.

The Steelers defense was toughening and Bledsoe was getting pressured. A momentum change was in the works. J. R. Redmond dropped a pass, and Gildon sacked Bledsoe on a three-and-out series.

The Steelers got a 28-yard return on a 38-yard punt by Ken Walter to the Patriots' 32. It took five plays and an untouched 11-yard run by Amos Zeroue to make this a too-close 21–17 game late in the third quarter.

Vinatieri nailed a 44-yard field goal early in the fourth quarter creating a touchdown advantage.

Threatening Bledsoe's triumphant return was a pass he wished he could take back, when he threw the ball directly into linebacker Joey Porter's hands. Only Porter's hands of stone saved Bledsoe from a rough play. Another time, Bledsoe was being pressured and he threw a pass behind his back like a basketball player, but no damage came of that one either.

Really, this wasn't Bledsoe at his best, but it was Bledsoe winning a game. He went 10 for 21 for 102 yards and one TD.

Helping matters was Jones' interception of Stewart, which foiled the Steelers' attempts to get close. Jones had such an unbelievable year. Big plays, big hits. At one time Bobby Grier and Pete Carroll, leaders of the former regime, were criticized for taking Jones in the first round. That was because they were playing him out of position at corner, when he always belonged at safety.

Vinatieri missed a 50-yarder wide left with 2:21 remaining, but the Patriots had this one. When Milloy intercepted Stewart late, this game was over. Bledsoe took a knee to end it.

"They just outplayed us—period," said Stewart, who had thrown one touchdown pass and eight interceptions in his four career games against New England. "Not so much me, but the entire offense."

Stewart, who motivated the Patriots with his mouth, couldn't help but comment, "Sometimes the best team doesn't win."

In the end, Milloy got his respect. Stewart went home, but to watch the Super Bowl, not play in it.

"You never disrespect anybody," said Milloy. "You just make it hard on yourself. I'm just surprised the veterans on that team didn't shut the younger guys' mouths. It was a momentum builder for us. We rallied around that, and in the end we were the AFC champions."

Belichick, two years on the job, got to the Super Bowl again, this time as the head coach, not Parcells' underling.

Kraft said of his coach, "I can say that Bill Belichick was worth everything we gave up to get him two years ago."

Kraft addressed the team after the victory, congratulating them on a great season. "This is the true meaning of *team*," said Kraft. "We never talk about individuals here."

On the field the scene was pandemonium. Players were hugging and raising "No. 1" fingers into the air.

"We did it, we did it, Mr. Kraft," screamed Otis Smith as the game ended and the field became a sea of Patriots.

McGinest, who revived his Patriots career late in the season and in the playoffs, was a force, making it very uncomfortable for Stewart all day. Late in the game he turned to the Pittsburgh fans and shouted, "Cancel those reservations!"

After the game ended, McGinest yelled, "We're going back again, and this time, we're gonna win it."

The Patriots donned their AFC championship T-shirts and caps. There was very little talk about the Rams, who had to play a tough game to beat the Eagles, 29–24. Even Mike Martz, happy the Rams were going to the Super Bowl again, wasn't too thrilled about the opponent.

"Oh, Bill [Belichick]," said Martz. "We won't get much sleep this week. It's quite a challenge offensively for us. He does so much. They do a great job of attacking what you do. The running game, and I think they are as well rounded and well coached in all three phases of the game as any team in the league."

Not long after the celebration, speculation abounded as to who would start at quarterback against St. Louis in New Orleans.

"Ah, let me enjoy this before you ask me that question," said Weis. "We just beat a great team."

CBS sports announcer Jim Nantz attempted the question with Belichick on national TV and got a similar answer: "We'll have to talk about that later, Jim."

Brady was riddled as well. He was walking better than he had been when he originally injured his ankle. He was walking close to normal, and that seemed to give an indication of what was to come.

Brady said, "I'm feeling good. I expect to play."

The Patriots returned to Boston after the game, deciding to get some "logistical things" done, according to Belichick, before heading to New Orleans. The events of September 11 had pushed everything back, eliminating, thankfully, that dreaded two-week period between the championship games and the Super Bowl.

The Patriots were back at the stadium at 8:00 A.M. on January 29, where they were briefed about tickets and reservations, all of the things the Steelers had done the week before. On their way to the airport for their charter flight to New Orleans, the team stopped at the State House in Boston for a brief ceremony in front of more than 1,000 fans. Governor Jane Swift introduced Kraft, who showed off the AFC championship trophy, while Belichick, Brown, and Milloy gave speeches.

When they got to New Orleans, the staff at the Fairmont Hotel had to scramble to take down all of the Pittsburgh Steelers preparations they had made. Even the hotel staff thought the Steelers would win. Just another motivating slap in the face for the Patriots.

CHAPTER 21

Here's a Story

Not long after Tom Brady had been drafted in the sixth round out of Michigan in April 2000, the young, skinny quarterback was going down a set of stairs in Smithfield, Rhode Island, when Kraft was coming up the same.

"He's holding a pizza box in his hands," recalled Kraft. "He's this tall, skinny kid and he extends his hand and says, 'Hi, Mr. Kraft, nice to meet you. I'm Tom Brady from Michigan.'

"I said, 'Nice to meet you, Tom.'

"He turns to me very seriously and says, 'Mr. Kraft, I'm the best decision your organization's ever made.'"

Kraft was bowled over. Pretty brash, he thought.

In the months and weeks to come he heard nothing but good things concerning Brady, a very studious kid who absorbed knowledge like a sponge.

Prior to Brady's first start against Indianapolis, Kraft recalls visiting with Brady on the field.

"Remember what you told me when I first met you?"

Brady nodded. "I sure do. Don't worry, I'll show you," said Brady.

Of course, Brady led the Patriots to a 44–13 win over the Colts, and the rest we've chronicled in depth in this book. Kraft and the Patriots coaching staff considered him a godsend. This is a kid who always impressed his coaches at every level but was never, say, in the "incredible athlete" category like his counterpart, Drew Henson.

At Serra High School in San Mateo, California, Brady had good numbers, but his teams had average records. Heck, he was dwarfed by the who's who that had come and gone at Serra long before he had arrived.

Last year alone, Serra High alumnus Barry Bonds clubbed 73 homers, the most ever in a single season; Lynn Swann, another alumnus, was inducted into the National Football League Hall of Fame; and Brady made his mark when he was named the Super Bowl MVP.

As Jim McCabe of the *Boston Globe* divulged in a piece on Brady's background, Brady invented a jump-roping drill that the Serra football program adopted. He was also a good enough athlete to be courted heavily by Cal, which really wanted him to stay close to home and which nearly got him to transfer from Michigan.

After visiting Michigan, however, Brady realized there was no other choice. Ann Arbor has called many to its hallowed grounds, and Brady fell in love with the campus, the tradition, and the football.

Brady could have forgone any temptation at big-time college football and played professional baseball. The Montreal Expos drafted him as a catcher. He could have demanded big money to sign. In a baseball tryout at the Kingdome as a senior, he'd wowed the scouts by hitting four out of the park. But even the baseball people knew they had no shot. He was a quarterback first, a catcher second, and there was no chance anyone was going to change his mind.

At Michigan he went through trying times. Only in his junior year was he the out-and-out choice as the starter. The previous years he had battled Brian Griese and lost. As a senior he had to split time with freshman phenom Henson, who eventually made the opposite choice—to play third base for the New York Yankees.

"I don't think anyone had to overcome more at Michigan than Tom," recalled Henson. "He worked so hard. He spent endless hours watching film. When game time rolled around, nobody was more prepared to play that game than Tom. I learned so much from him. What he went through at Michigan prepared him for what lay ahead with the Patriots."

It was the constant fighting for his job that seemed to harden Brady. Though a nice, quiet kid on the exterior, the interior was something quite different. He possessed a competitive desire and the fire to be the best. There was a quiet cockiness within him. As soon as his physical tools caught up with his mental tools, Brady was able to back up his desires on the field.

"I like to think I made Tom a better quarterback because of the competition I provided," said Henson. "I can say that Tom made me better because he fought so hard for his job."

As a junior Brady completed 61.1 percent of his passes for 2,638 yards and 15 touchdowns in leading the Wolverines to a 10–3 record.

But when Brady was a senior, Henson was ready. Henson was the local hero, a superstar from Brighton, Michigan. Michigan coach Lloyd Carr decided to let Brady start and Henson come in in the second quarter. In the second half Carr would go with the hot hand. Brady was usually the second-half starter, but against Michigan State, Carr went with Henson. Henson threw a costly interception and Michigan trailed 27–10 before Carr went back to Brady. As much as he tried to rally them back, they lost, 34–31. But after that game Brady became the full-time starter again, leading the Wolverines to five straight wins to finish at 10–2.

"There was no resentment on my part," recalled Henson. "I knew coach Carr had to make a decision at that point, and Tom was older and I knew I was going to be there next year. Coach Carr made the right choice. I just supported Tom in any way I could, just as he supported me. I have to say that even though I came in and took his job for a while, he handled it so well. Being a few years older, he always helped me with whatever situation I faced."

Brady ended his collegiate career with a 35–34 upset win over Alabama. He completed 34 for 46 for 369 yards and four touchdowns.

It's funny how things worked out. Brady went on to be the Super Bowl MVP and the youngest quarterback to ever win a Super Bowl. Henson, who would have been the No. 1 draft pick of the Houston Texans in the April draft had he stayed with football, is now hoping to leave Triple-A Columbus and make it as the Yankees' third baseman sometime during the 2002 baseball season.

"I think I live vicariously through Tom, and I think he lives vicariously through me," said Henson. "Even though I've chosen baseball, I've wondered what it was like to win a Super Bowl because I'll never have that experience, and Tom has wondered what it's like to be a professional baseball player."

Henson said he spoke to Brady two or three times during his incredible journey, and he made this observation: "Each time I spoke to him I could sense his level of confidence rising. I spoke to him in training camp and he was happy with the progress he'd made. Then I spoke to him when he first replaced Drew Bledsoe, and he hoped he could just keep the seat warm and play well. Then when Bill Belichick named him the quarterback, you could just sense what that did for Tom. His confidence just shot through the roof, and he didn't let anyone down."

Henson said he was shocked in some ways by Brady's leading the Patriots but in other ways not.

"I was shocked in that Tom didn't have any NFL starting experience," said Henson. "How can you go from fourth-string to second-string and then starting and play like that? He always said that if you take care of the football and do things the right way that you'll always find someone open to get the ball to. If you look at his season and what he did, that was so true. He took care of the football and took what the defense gave him. He was smart. He didn't try to be a hero and force the ball."

* * *

Brady sat in his booth on Media Day at the Superdome on Tuesday, January 29, with no boot, crutches, or cast supporting his sore left ankle.

"We've got to practice to play, and I anticipate being out there ready to practice to play. It's not as big of a deal to me as it is to a lot of people. You go out there, and as Coach says, 'You just suck it up.' I know if you want to play, you've got to practice," said Brady.

The kid always said the right thing. He always showed a desire to play, hurt or not hurt. He said he never received a cortisone shot or any foreign substance to make the ankle feel better. Good, old-fashioned Mother Nature healed it. Spit on it, and let's go.

Down at the farthest end from Brady, Bledsoe dodged a collage of questions concerning whether he'd play. Reporters were asking the same question umpteen different ways. Bledsoe would sometimes comment, "That's a pretty creative way to ask."

It was clear that Belichick needed only to see Brady perform without incident in practice. He would look for good flexibility and movement in the ankle and good mechanics on his throws. He needed to see that Brady would not be a hindrance to the team on the field because of restrictions.

After all, Brady was Belichick's man. It was nice what Bledsoe did against Pittsburgh, but it was no secret that Belichick preferred Brady, whom he thought gave the Patriots the best chance to win.

"I want to play," said Bledsoe. "I want to play more than anything I've ever wanted in my life. After sitting there for so long, I got a little taste, but it doesn't satisfy my hunger. My love for the game has never wavered. Nor has my confidence in what I can do."

On January 30, after watching Brady go through practice at Tulane University, Belichick declared Brady fit to play.

"Tom demonstrated in practice that he is fit to play," said Belichick, through pool reporter Peter King of *Sports Illustrated*, the only media rep allowed to witness practice. "He'll be our starting quarterback on Sunday."

Belichick made a thorough decision. After practice, he and the coaches viewed video of that day's practice session to make sure their eyes were telling them the truth. They found that Brady had good movement, threw the ball well, and wasn't inhibited.

Later, Belichick met with Brady, then Bledsoe, to tell them the news individually.

Bledsoe described the parlay as "brief." He was disappointed.

As he left the hotel that night for a bite to eat, Butch Stearns of Fox Sports Channel 25 in Boston caught up to him. He told Stearns, "I'm very disappointed. I wanted to play, but I'll support Tom as I have the entire season."

Kraft made some headlines on January 30 as well. When asked about the quarterback situation he said, "I wouldn't be against both being here unless someone comes up with a blockbuster offer for either one."

It was a comment that could be twisted and turned and interpreted a number of different ways. Kraft said his opinion was that of a fan and that the ultimate decision would rest with Belichick.

"I've had the privilege of knowing Drew Bledsoe for eight years," said Kraft. "He's the prototype anyone would want on their football team. He's in a different situation right now and it must be difficult for him. But right now it's about winning the biggest game of the season and that's Bill's call."

This was Kraft's second appearance as an owner at the Super Bowl in New Orleans.

"The last time we came here I felt more like an adolescent," said Kraft. "Now I feel more like a mature adult because I understand how difficult it is to get here. I feel privileged to be here."

Kraft spoke glowingly of Belichick. He recalled the first time he met him, in 1996, how well organized and informed he was.

"I'll never forget that he had notes on virtually every player. He was able to trace Chris Slade, for example, from his high school years to the present. He's a combination student-professor," said Kraft.

The Patriots owner never revealed why he didn't hire Belichick right off the bat after Parcells' exit. While Parcells was absent from the 1996 plane ride home from New Orleans to New England, Kraft had a chance to speak to Belichick, but he never offered him the job. Instead Kraft went on a coaching hunt, offering the job to George Seifert, who turned it down, and then settling on Pete Carroll.

Kraft said he followed Belichick's coaching when he went to the Jets and was impressed by the defensive schemes, especially against the Patriots. When the kinder, gentler approach of Carroll had run its course after three years, Kraft knew whom he wanted, and Belichick got the call.

After a rough start to his career, Belichick soon began to get the type of players he wanted, and coaching them became easier.

"He sees the game at a different speed than most of us," said linebacker coach Rob Ryan, whose father is the incomparable Buddy Ryan of Chicago Bears fame. "Being around my father, I've now had a chance to work with two of the best defensive minds in the game. There are some similarities in how they know how to attack the other teams' weaknesses."

Dante Scarnecchia, who has survived every administration since 1982, said of Belichick, "He is so thorough. Each morning he comes in and says here are three or four things you need to touch on today, and sometimes it involves something he's seen in practice the day before."

Added Ryan, "The way he manages his time is unbelievable."

* * *

Part of the fun of covering the Super Bowl is watching Patriots fans in this venue. I noticed during the week that Rams fans were a little better behaved and carried a quiet Midwestern confidence.

They knew their team was superior.

Patriots fans were louder, but it seemed they were out in greater numbers. Much like the team they rooted for, Patriots fans had a bit of a chip on their shoulder. From the looks of it, they'd been disrespected about as much as the team.

When a Patriots fan on a horse-drawn buggy spotted a Rams fan down Decatur, he yelled, "We're going home with the championship!"

Replied the Rams fan, "Championship? When's the last time you guys won one of those? Boston's a bunch of losers."

Ouch. Boston fans are very sensitive about the lack of championships for their sports teams (other than the Celtics of course).

The Patriots fan ordered the buggy to be stopped and was ready to go after the man, but he stopped himself. He looked down at the Rams fan and said, "You're gonna be crying on Sunday night. You're gonna be crying," pointing a finger, that at that moment, looked like a dagger.

Another time a fellow was in a store trying to purchase some Patriots garb, and the clerk said to him, "I recommend the Rams gear. They're gonna win the game." The Patriots fan walked out.

Disrespect for the Patriots was everywhere.

With the Patriots 14-point underdogs in Vegas, a lot of people made big money on this one. But it was clear to not only the team but also the fans who gathered in the Big Easy that week that nobody really took them seriously.

The rows of radio talk shows at the convention center babbled 24-7 about this one-sided game. *USA Today* printed lopsided picks by the national media, although many writers in the Boston area were looking for an upset, including yours truly, picking a 24–21 score. Two Boston sportscasters, Bob Lobel at Channel 4, the CBS affiliate, and Chris Collins of New England Cable News, picked the score right on the nose.

As the week progressed, the majority thinking may have been softening a bit. The national media got to meet the team at daily press conferences, and soon there was a sense that there might be something special about this team.

A team of destiny?

They were not a team of superstars, for sure, but every player had a specific role. How many teams do you know where the players hit the specifications of their roles so precisely? Not many. Just the ones who defy all odds. It was the ultimate in teamwork. Near perfect.

"There is an old saying about the strength of the wolf in the pack and I think there's lot of truth to that," said Belichick during the season. "On a football team, it's not the strength of the individual players, but it's the strength of the unit and how they all function together."

* * *

On February 4, more than 1.25 million fans gathered for a celebratory rally at Government Center in Boston along a congested parade route. Patriots players were aboard duck vehicles, waving to the crowd, which was 10-people deep in places along the side of the road in subfreezing temperatures.

There was talk that if the Red Sox had ever won there'd be twice as many people. Maybe so. But the Red Sox have kept their fans waiting 84 years, and this was the football team's moment, an example to our children and to all mankind that anything is possible.

Belichick warned that the entire team wouldn't be back for 2002 when the Patriots, who played in the worst facility in the NFL, moved into their new digs at CMGI Field, a true reward for their accomplishments. Through March, the Patriots had already signed Seattle free-agent tight end Christian Fauria, Carolina Panthers wide receiver Donald Hayes, former Saints safety Rob Kelly and tight end Cam Cleeland, and Jets defensive lineman Rick Lyle and special teamer Chris Hayes. They had re-signed Antowain Smith and Vinatieri to long-term deals.

On April 1, several players threw out the ceremonial first pitch at the Boston Red Sox's season opener against the Toronto Blue Jays, and the next day they were honored by President Bush at the Rose Garden at the White House.

Director of player personnel Scott Pioli was active on April 20 during the draft, making a trade with Washington to move up 11 spots and take University of Colorado tight end Daniel Graham—hopefully ending the revolving door of ineffective tight ends that has plagued New England since Ben Coates was released following the 1999 season.

But the biggest off season news came the next day—April 21—when the Patriots traded Bledsoe to rival Buffalo for a number-one draft pick in 2003.

After weeks of on again, off again trade negotiations with the Bills, and rumors that the deal might be dead, the Patriots, who had held out for a first-round pick, had no qualms about dealing Bledsoe to the rising Bills.

One league executive, who wished to stay anonymous, said, "The word on the Patriots is they don't think Bledsoe can play at a high level anymore. They think they can stop him when they face him twice a year."

Though Belichick owned a 5–4 record against Bledsoe while head coach of Cleveland and defensive coordinator with the Jets, we shall see.

The Red Sox made a similar decision at the end of the 1996 season when they allowed Roger Clemens to sign with the Toronto Blue Jays, feeling he could no longer pitch at a high level. He went on to win three Cy Youngs and two World Series rings with the New York Yankees.

Bledsoe decided to take the high road after the deal was made, leaving the organization as he left it, with class and dignity. "I'm not going to say anything bad about anyone," Bledsoe said. "The rivalry with the Patriots is going to be fun, as long as both teams are in the hunt for the playoffs. I have nothing but the best memories of New England. It's hard to believe it's over."

Maybe the 2002 version of this team will forge its own identity, for there will never be another team like the 2001 Patriots.

The Super Bowl XXXVI champs were a team that began its quest with few expectations. Every week the players were fighting "the unbeatable foe." Every week they got closer to reaching for a star, "no matter how hopeless, and no matter how far." They fought to be respected and treated seriously "without question or pause."

This Impossible Team had a quest, to follow their gut, their heart, their will toward the unthinkable and the improbable—a Super Bowl championship.

Afterword

I t's time to move on to a new season with a whole new set of circumstances. But I'll never forget what happened on February 3, 2002, at the Superdome in New Orleans. How could I?

I remember Johnny Hillebrand—we call him "Johnny Rotten"—our equipment guy, was standing right next to me when the Rams tied the game (17–17). I basically said to him, "The Rams screwed up; they left too much time on the clock." At that point I ran toward the (practice) net because I figured about 90 percent of the time, unless someone breaks loose for a touchdown, you get into position to kick a field goal.

I pretty much knew if the offense got in range it was going to come down to my foot.

Everything happened so fast, I didn't have time to think about it. I'd be lying if I said for years and years I thought about making the winning field goal in the Super Bowl, and I probably dreamt that a hundred times in my sleep the night before.

You march on the field and go. I wasn't as nervous as I thought I would be at that point.

From the time I started working in the net to the time I stepped out on the field, I don't think anybody said anything to me. It was as if I had the plague at that point.

When you're lining up and you have a chance to kick the game winner, everybody pretty much leaves you alone to do your thing.

Kicking for me is like a golf shot is for golfers—most of the time I know if I hit it well. Sometimes it doesn't go where you think it's going to go, but that one felt good leaving my foot.

When I looked up and saw it going straight I knew I was going to have plenty of distance. I was probably jumping up and down and celebrating with my hands in the air long before it went through the uprights.

It's all about timing and elevation, which is usually good in a dome. I have faith in the guys up front that they're going to block for me. They're the unsung heroes up front. They basically get bowled over, but they all hung in there. I never have to worry about getting blocked.

I remember there were seven seconds left on the clock before the kick and I really thought, when it left my foot and went through the uprights, I thought there were going to be a couple of seconds left on the clock. So I'm thinking I've got to go back to the sideline and grab my tee and kick off. Next thing I know (punter and holder) Ken Walter is jumping at me yelling, "We just won the Super Bowl! We just won the Super Bowl!" There were a few cusswords, but I won't add them. At that point I could hear the "We Are the Champions" song and the confetti was coming down. I realized the time had expired. Everybody was running around, hugging, and just unbelievable emotion at that point.

Was I surprised? No. I thought back to training camp. Every year the team is comprised of different guys, but I thought coach Belichick and the front office did a great job bringing in good football players and good guys on the team. Once we got into training camp and we were practicing against the defending NFC champion New York Giants, I thought to myself, "We can play with these guys." I thought we were as good as they were and possibly better. That was a good sign.

Once we came back from adversity in the Chargers game and won, we had that ability. Then when we beat Indianapolis in

Indianapolis I thought we were a better football team than people were giving us credit for being.

Of course, it's easy to say that, but we had to prove it the rest of the way. We did.

It was an amazing year. The opportunities we all had to contribute something were right in front of us, and we all took advantage of them.

This year I had five game-winning field goals. Some years you may have only one, or maybe none. We had so many close games.

Stepping on the field for that field goal in the Super Bowl, I felt so fortunate to contribute in my role. Whenever we had adversity someone would step up and make a big play. At that point guys had been making plays all year, and I said to myself, "This is your turn to make one."

What we did, when I think back, was amazing. To do it one time is hard; to repeat is harder because everyone is trying to knock you off. Your schedule is tougher.

No matter how many times we win it, the first time will be the most special because it was something that had never happened before. It's not that it wouldn't be extremely special again.

I know one thing, we definitely earned the right to say we were the world champions.

In all the sports and in all the years I've played, I've never been so proud to be a part of something as this. Guys didn't care about their personal goals and personal achievements.

Wherever I go, people comment about how we all came out together as a team to start the Super Bowl and where that started. I told them that's something we did early in the season because it felt right. We have a bunch of great guys who worked so well together, and we wanted to show the world that we were the ultimate team.

We had so much veteran leadership, from Bryan Cox to Drew Bledsoe. To do what we did, we had to come together as a team. It started when Bledsoe went down and Tom Brady came in.

I think the guys felt they had to step up and help Tom out and give him as much support as possible. At that point the offensive line, the running backs, and the receivers decided they were going to help Tom develop his confidence. All of them elevated their play and they came together as a team.

But even when we won the Super Bowl, I'm not sure we had the respect. When Baltimore won it, everyone said, "What a great defense they have." With us, it's "Oh, they were lucky." The analysts have already come out for next year and told us we're a "middle of the pack" team. To be the best you've got to beat the best. We beat Oakland, Pittsburgh, and the Rams. I'm not sure what more we have to do.

It's funny. Earlier in the season we started this "don't talk to me" kind of thing on the team. It started as an ongoing joke, but then as the year went along there were people and reporters and analysts who didn't think we'd amount to much and who thought we'd win six or eight games because Drew was hurt. We decided to take the stand, "If that's the way you feel, I don't have anything to say to you. Don't come over and ask some stupid questions. Don't ask us questions and then disrespect us later on." Lawyer (Milloy) and Ty (Law) were pissed. They and all of us adopted a "we're gonna show you" mantra.

I'd also like to say, our fans were amazing. This is the only team I ever played for, but our fans stuck with us through thick and thin. To have 1.2 million people in Boston at the parade the next day and 60,000–70,000 in Providence supporting us was something I'll never forget.

I don't think I saw one empty seat in the Oakland game. To sit in a snowstorm to watch a game . . . I'm not sure many other fans would have done that.

We all felt so good for the fans because for 42 years the Patriots hadn't given them a championship. I can't tell you how many letters I received that had the same message: "I can die a happy man now."

—Adam Vinatieri
April 8, 2002

Index